THE PROBLEM
OF THE
UNEMPLOYED

AN ENQUIRY AND
AN ECONOMIC POLICY

WITH AN
INTRODUCTORY CHAPTER
FROM
Problems of Poverty

By

J. A. HOBSON

First published in 1896

This edition published by Read Books Ltd.
Copyright © 2019 Read Books Ltd.
This book is copyright and may not be
reproduced or copied in any way without
the express permission of the publisher in writing

British Library Cataloguing-in-Publication Data
A catalogue record for this book is available
from the British Library

MORAL
ASPECTS OF POVERTY

A CHAPTER FROM
Problems Of Poverty
BY JOHN ATKINSON HOBSON

§ 1. "Moral" View of the Causes of Poverty.—Our diagnosis of "sweating" has regarded poverty as an industrial disease, and we have therefore concerned ourselves with the examination of industrial remedies, factory legislation, Trade Unionism, and restrictions of the supply of unskilled labour. It may seem that in doing this we have ignored certain important moral factors in the problem, which, in the opinion of many, are all important. Until quite recently the vast majority of those philanthropic persons who interested themselves in the miserable conditions of the poor, paid very slight attention to the economic aspect of poverty, and never dreamed of the application of economic remedies. It is not unnatural that religions and moral teachers engaged in active detailed work among the poor should be so strongly impressed by the moral symptoms of the disease as to mistake them for the prime causes. "It is a fact apparent to every thoughtful man that the larger portion of the misery that constitutes our Social Question arises from idleness, gluttony, drink, waste, indulgence, profligacy, betting, and dissipation." These words of Mr. Arnold White express the common view of those philanthropists who do not understand what is meant by "the industrial system," and of the bulk of the comfortable classes when they are confronted with the evils of poverty as disclosed in "the sweating system." Intemperance, unthrift, idleness, and inefficiency are indeed common vices of the poor. If therefore we could teach the poor to be temperate, thrifty, industrious, and efficient, would not the problem of poverty be solved? Is not a moral remedy instead of an economic remedy the one to be desired? The question at issue here is a vital one to all who earnestly desire to secure a better life for the poor. This "moral view" has much to recommend it at first sight. In the first place, it is a "moral" view, and as morality is admittedly the truest and most real end of man, it would seem that a moral cure must be more radical and efficient than any merely industrial cure. Again, these "vices" of the poor, drink, dirt, gambling, prostitution, &c., are very definite and concrete maladies attaching to large numbers of individual cases, and visibly responsible for the misery and degradation of the vicious and their families. Last, not least, this aspect of poverty, by representing the condition of the poor to be chiefly "their own fault," lightens the sense of responsibility for the "well to do." It is decidedly the more comfortable view, for it at once flatters the pride of the rich by representing poverty as an evidence of incompetency, salves his conscience when pricked by the contrast of the misery around him, and assists him to secure his material interests by adopting an attitude of stern repression towards large industrial or political agitations in the interests of labour, on the ground that "these are wrong ways of tackling the question."

§ 2. "Unemployment" and the Vices of the Poor.—The question is this, Can the poor be moralized, and will that cure Poverty? To discuss this question with the fullness it deserves is here impossible, but the following considerations will furnish some data for an answer—

In the first place, it is very difficult to ascertain to what extent drink, vice, idleness, and other personal defects are actually responsible for poverty in individual cases. There is, however, reason to believe that the bulk of cases of extreme poverty and destitution cannot be traced to these personal vices, but, on the other hand, that they are attributable to industrial causes for which the sufferer is not responsible. The following is the result of a careful analysis of 4000 cases of "very poor" undertaken by Mr. Charles Booth. These are grouped as follows according to the apparent causes of distress—

- 4 per cent, are "loafers."
- 14 " " are attributed to drink and thriftlessness.
- 27 " " are due to illness, large families, or other misfortunes.
- 55 " " are assigned to "questions of employment."

Here, in the lowest class of city poor, moral defects are the direct cause of distress in only 18 per cent. of the cases, though doubtless they may have acted as contributory or indirect causes in a larger number.

In the classes just above the "very poor," 68 per cent. of poverty is attributed to "questions of employment," and only 13 per cent. to drink and thriftlessness. In the lowest parts of Whitechapel drink figures very slightly, affecting only 4 per cent. of the very poor, and 1 per cent. of the poor, according to Mr. Booth. Even applied to a higher grade of labour, a close investigation of facts discloses a grossly exaggerated notion of the sums spent in drink by city workers in receipt of good wages. A careful inquiry into the expenditure of a body of three hundred Amalgamated Engineers during a period of two years, yielded an average of 1s. 9d. per week spent on drink.

So, too, in the cases brought to the notice of the Lords' Committee, drink and personal vices do not play the most important part. The Rev. S. A. Barnett, who knows East London so well, does not find the origin of poverty in the vices of the poor. Terrible as are the results of drunkenness, impurity, unthrift, idleness, disregard of sanitary rules, it is not possible, looking fairly at the facts, to regard these as the main sources of poverty. If we are not carried away by the spirit of some special fanaticism, we shall look upon these evils as the natural and necessary accessories of the struggle for a livelihood, carried on under the industrial conditions of our age and country. Even supposing it were demonstrable that a much larger proportion of the cases of poverty and misery were the direct consequence of these moral and sanitary vices of the poor, we should not be justified in concluding that moral influence and education were the most effectual cures, capable of direct application. It is indeed highly probable that the "unemployed" worker is on the average morally and industrially inferior to the "employed," and from the individual point of view this inferiority is often responsible for his non-employment. But this only means that differences of moral and industrial character determine what particular individuals shall succeed or fail in the fight for work and wages. It by no means follows that if by education we could improve all these moral and industrial weaklings they could obtain steady employment without displacing others. Where an over-supply of labour exists, no remedy which does not operate either by restricting the supply or increasing the demand for labour can be effectual.

§ 3. **Civilization ascends from Material to Moral.**—The life of the poorest and most degraded classes is impenetrable to the highest influences of civilization. So long as the bare struggle for continuance of physical existence absorbs all their energies, they cannot be civilized. The consideration of the greater intrinsic worth of the moral life than the merely physical life, must not be allowed to mislead us. That which has the precedence in value has not the precedence in time. We must begin with the lower life before we can ascend to the higher. As in the individual the *corpus sanum* is rightly an object of earlier solicitude in education than the *mens sana*, though the latter may be of higher importance; so with the progress of a class. We cannot go to the lowest of our slum population and teach them to be clean, thrifty, industrious, steady, moral, intellectual, and religious, until we have first taught them how to secure for themselves the industrial conditions of healthy physical life. Our poorest classes have neither the time, the energy, or the desire to be clean, thrifty, intellectual, moral, or religious. In our haste we forget that there is a proper and necessary order in the awakening of desires. At present our "slum" population do not desire to be moral and intellectual, or even to be particularly clean. Therefore these higher goods must wait, so far as they are dependent on the voluntary action of the poor. What these people do want is better food, and more of it; warmer clothes; better and surer shelter; and greater security of permanent employment on decent wages. Until we can assist them to gratify these "lower" desires, we shall try in vain to awaken "higher" ones. We must prepare the soil of a healthy physical existence before we can hope to sow the moral seed so as to bring forth fruit. Upon a sound physical foundation alone can we build a high moral and spiritual civilization.

Moral and sanitary reformers have their proper sphere of action among those portions of the working classes who have climbed the first rounds in the ladder of civilization, and stand on tolerably firm conditions of material comfort and security. They cannot hope at present to achieve any great success among the poorest workers. The fact must not be shirked that in preaching thrift, hygiene, morality, and religion to the dwellers in the courts and alleys of our great cities, we are sowing seed upon a barren ground. Certain isolated cases of success must not blind us to this truth. Take, for example, thrift. It is not possible to expect that large class of workers who depend upon irregular earnings of less than 18s. a week to set by anything for a rainy day. The essence of thrift is regularity, and regularity is to them impossible. Even supposing their scant wage was regular, it is questionable whether they would be justified in stinting the bodily necessities of their families by setting aside a portion which could not in the long run suffice to provide even a bare maintenance for old age or disablement. To say this is not to impugn the value of thrift in maintaining a character of dignity and independence in the worker; it is simply to recognize that valuable as these qualities are, they must be subordinated to the first demands of physical life. Those who can save without encroaching on the prime necessaries of life ought to save; but there are still many who cannot save, and these are they whom the problem of poverty especially concerns. The saying of Aristotle, that "it is needful first to have a maintenance, and then to practise virtue," does not indeed imply that we *ought* to postpone practising the moral virtues until we have secured ourselves against want, but rather means that before we can live well we *must* first be able to live at all.

Precisely the same is true of the "inefficiency" of the poor. Nothing is more common than to hear men and women, often incapable themselves of earning by work the money which they spend, assigning as the root of poverty the inefficiency of the poor. It is quite true that the "poor" consist for the most part of inefficient workers. It would be strange if it were not so. How shall a child of the slums, ill-fed in body and mind, brought up in the industrial and moral degradation of low city life, without a chance of learning how to use hands or head, and to acquire habits of steady industry, become an efficient workman? The conditions under which they grow up to manhood and womanhood preclude the possibility of efficiency. It is the bitterest portion of the lot of the poor that they are deprived of the opportunity of learning to work well. To taunt them with their incapacity, and to regard it as the cause of poverty, is nothing else than a piece of blind insolence. Here and there an individual may be to blame for neglected opportunities; but the "poor" as a class have no more chance under present conditions of acquiring "efficiency" than of attaining to refined artistic taste, or the culminating Christian virtue of holiness. Inefficiency is one of the worst and most degrading aspects of poverty; but to regard it as the leading cause is an error fatal to a true understanding of the problem.

We now see why it is impossible to seriously entertain the claim of Co-operative Production as a direct remedy for poverty. The success of Co-operative schemes depends almost entirely upon the presence of high moral and intellectual qualities in those co-operating—trust, patience, self restraint, and obedience combined with power of organization, skill, and business enterprise. These qualities are not yet possessed by our skilled artisan class to the extent requisite to enable them to readily succeed in productive co-operation; how can it be expected then that low-skilled inefficient labour should exhibit them? The enthusiastic co-operator says we must educate them up to the requisite moral and intellectual level. The answer is, that it is impossible to apply such educating influences effectually, until we have first placed them on a sound physical basis of existence; that is to say, until we have already cured the worst form of the malady. From whatever point we approach this question we are driven to the conclusion that as the true cause of the disease is an industrial one, so the earliest remedies must be rather industrial than moral or educational.

§ 4. **Effects of Temperance and Technical Education.**— Again, we are by no means justified in leaping to the conclusion that if we could induce workers to become more sober, more industrious, or more skilful, their industrial condition would of necessity be improved to a corresponding extent. If we can induce an odd farm-labourer here and there to give up his "beer," he and his family are no doubt better off to the extent of this saving, and can employ the money in some much more profitable way. But if the whole class of farm-labourers could be persuaded to become teetotalers without substituting some new craving of equal force in the place of drink, it is extremely probable that in all places where there was an abundant supply of farm-labourers, the wage of a farm-labourer would gradually fall to the extent of the sum of money formerly spent in beer. For the lowest paid classes of labourers get, roughly speaking, no more wages than will just suffice to provide them with what they insist on regarding as necessaries of life. To an ordinary labourer "beer" is a part of the minimum subsistence for less than which he will not consent to work at all. Where there is an abundance of labour, as is generally the case in low-skilled employments, this minimum subsistence or lowest standard of comfort practically determines wages. If you were merely to take something away from this recognized minimum without putting something else to take its place, you would actually lower the rate of wages. If, by a crusade of temperance pure and simple, you made teetotalers of the mass of low-skilled workers, their wages would indisputably fall, although they might be more competent workers than before. If, on the other hand, following the true line of temperance reform, you expelled intemperance by substituting for drink some healthier, higher, and equally strong desire which cost as much or more to attain its satisfaction; if in giving up drink they insisted on providing against sickness and old age, or upon better houses and more recreation and enjoyment, then their wages would not fall, and might even rise in proportion as their new wants, as a class, were more expensive than the craving for drink which they had abandoned.

Or, again, take the case of technical or general education. In so far as technical education enabled a number of men who would otherwise have been unskilled labourers, to compete for skilled work, it will no doubt enable these men to raise themselves in the industrial sense; but the addition of their number to the ranks of skilled labour will imply an increase in supply of skilled labour, and a decrease in supply of unskilled labour; the price or wage for unskilled labour will rise, but the wage for skilled labour will fall assuming the relationship between the demand for skilled and unskilled labour to remain as before. A mere increase in the efficiency of labour, though it would increase the quantity of wealth produced, and render a rise of wages possible, would of itself have no economic force to bring about a rise. No improvement in the character of labour will be effectual in raising wages unless it causes a rise in the standard of comfort, which he demands as a condition of the use of his labour. If we merely increased the efficiency of labour without a corresponding stimulation of new wants, we should be simply increasing the mass of labour-power offered for sale, and the price of each portion would fall correspondingly. It would confer no more *direct* benefit upon the worker as such, than does the introduction of some new machine which has the same effect of adding to the average efficiency of the worker. Those who would advocate technical and general education, with a view to the material improvement of the masses, must see that this education be applied in such a way as to assist in implanting and strengthening new wholesome demands in those educated, so as to effectively raise this standard of living. There can be little doubt but that such education would create new desires, and so would indirectly secure the industrial elevation of the masses. But it ought to be clearly recognized that the industrial force which operates *directly* to raise the wages of the workers, is not technical skill, or increased efficiency of labour, but the elevated standard of comfort required by the working-classes. It is at the same time true, that if we could merely stimulate the workers to new wants requiring higher wages, they could not necessarily satisfy all these new wants. If it were possible to induce all labourers to demand such increase of wages as sufficed to enable them to lay by savings, it is difficult to say whether they could in all cases press this claim successfully. But if at the same time their efficiency as labourers likewise grew, it will be evident that they both can and would raise that standard of living.

In so far as the results of technical education upon the class of low-skilled labourers alone is concerned, it is evident that it would relieve the constant pressure of an excessive supply. Whatever the effect of this might be upon the industrial condition of the skilled industries subjected to the increased competition, there can be no doubt that the wages of low-skilled labour would rise. Since the condition of unskilled or low-skilled workers forms the chief ingredient in poverty, such a "levelling up" may be regarded as a valuable contribution towards a cure of the worst phase of the disease.

This brief investigation of the working of moral and educational cures for industrial diseases shows us that these remedies can only operate in improving the material condition of the poorest classes, in so far as they conduce to raise the standard of living among the poor. Since a higher standard of comfort means economically a restriction in the number of persons willing to undertake work for a lower rate of wage than will support this standard of comfort, it may be said that moral remedies can be only effectual in so far as they limit the supply of low-skilled, low-paid labour. Thus we are brought round again to the one central point in the problem of poverty, the existence of an excessive supply of cheap labour.

§ 5. **The False Dilemma which impedes Progress.**—There are those who seek to retard all social progress by a false and mischievous dilemma which takes the following shape. No radical improvement in industrial organization, no work of social reconstruction, can be of any real avail unless it is preceded by such moral and intellectual improvement in the condition of the mass of workers as shall render the new machinery effective; unless the change in human nature comes first, a change in external conditions will be useless. On the other hand, it is evident that no moral or intellectual education can be brought effectively to bear upon the mass of human beings, whose whole energies are necessarily absorbed by the effort to secure the means of bare physical support. Thus it is made to appear as if industrial and moral progress must each precede the other, a thing which is impossible. Those who urge that the two forms of improvement must proceed *pari passu*, do not precisely understand what they propose.

The falsehood of the above dilemma consists in the assumption that industrial reformers wish to proceed by a sudden leap from an old industrial order to a new one. Such sudden movements are not in accordance with the gradual growth which nature insists upon as the condition of wise change. But it is equally in accordance with nature that the material growth precedes the moral. Not that the work of moral reconstruction can lag far behind. Each step in this industrial advancement of the poor should, and must, if the gain is to be permanent, be followed closely and secured by a corresponding advance in moral and intellectual character and habits. But the moral and religious reformer should never forget that in order of time material reform comes first, and that unless proper precedence be yielded to it, the higher ends of humanity are unattainable.

PREFACE

THE Unemployed Question has greatly suffered from the modern tendency of economic investigation in England to devote an almost exclusive attention to the study of detailed facts, ignoring the larger facts or principles in which these smaller facts find their unity. It may be readily conceded that the treatment of no industrial subject has suffered more than this from vague and unfounded generalities, and that the close labour of historical research in collecting and grouping facts is a most urgent need. Such work to be effective requires a separate investigation and discussion of the several forms and aspects of Unemployment and of the forces which are engaged in causing it. So the Unemployed Question easily bifurcates into the treatment of skilled and unskilled, able-bodied and inefficient, temporarily unemployed and surplus labour, country and town labour, while each trade is found to have its special characters and causes of seasonal irregularity or wider fluctuations.

But the need of this segmentary search for facts does not justify the common suggestion that there is not one Unemployed Problem but fifty, and that each must be treated entirely by itself upon the basis of its special facts, without reference to wider or more general principles.

The tendency thus to fritter away the unity of a great subject into an ever-widening number of component parts is a grave intellectual danger which induces a paralysis of all work of practical reform. My object in this book is to show that the Unemployed Question has a true unity which is clearly discernible amid the facts which are already ascertained, and which is inevitably hidden by the sectional treatment. After making due allowance for minor contributory causes, I claim to establish the identity of Unemployment as an aspect of Trade Depression and by further analysis of facts to establish Under-consumption as the direct economic cause of the industrial malady. The refusal to recognise that Industry both in volume and character, is directly determined by the effective demand of Consumers, with due allowance for the prophetic or stimulative influence of Producers, is still the deepest source of error in the English theory of the structure of Industry.

The identification of Unemployment with Under-consumption demands an explanation of that failure of Consumption to keep pace with Producing-power which is recognised as a general feature of industry in highly developed countries. This explanation is found in causes which affect the distribution of power to consume and induce individuals to endeavour to capitalise "unearned" elements of income at a greater pace than is economically needed to satisfy the demands of current consumption.

This economic analysis of the phenomena of Trade Depressions does not claim to be new in substance. Several early economists, in particular Lauderdale and

Malthus, gave a brilliant and a sound analysis of these phenomena, which was never refuted. Their valid arguments were rejected not because they were disproved, but because they were associated with views and practical proposals often rightly regarded as misleading or mischievous. The general acceptance of illogical and inconsistent definitions of the terms Capital and Demand, and a neglect to study the actual mechanism of Saving, have caused the main body of English professional economists to evade all scientific recognition of the phenomenon of an excess of general producing-power which is visible in periods of trade depression. No sufficient consideration has been accorded to several recent statements of the case, both in England and in the United States. In the latter country Mr. Uriel Crocker of Boston was the first to apply clearly and effectively this analysis to the modern phenomena of "depressed trade" in advanced industrial communities, and his latest statement entitled "*Hard Times*" is by far the most convincing short popular rendering of the argument. Mr. J. M. Robertson in his "*Fallacy of Saving*" gave a powerful reading of one important aspect of the case, the false or "*bogus*" saving which a futile endeavour to establish excessive capital engenders. Some years ago in conjunction with the late Mr. A. F. Mummery I endeavoured, in *The Physiology of Industry*, to call attention to the large issues involved in this line of thought. Several other writers * during recent years have effectively exposed the fallacies of Adam Smith's doctrine of Parsimony and J. S. Mill's Fundamental Propositions concerning Capital,

* *E.g.*, R. S. Moffat in "The Economy of Consumption." Frank Fairman, in various pamphlets. Dr. Hertzka in "Freeland." See also "The Evolution of Modern Capitalism", by the present writer.

though the force of their criticism in some instances is weakened by a disparagement of the habit of individual thrift, which is not rightly involved in the line of their attack and which indicates a failure to grasp the true relations between individual and social "saving." Their arguments have received little attention, in this country or in America, from the main body of economists, who still lean with childlike confidence upon a theory of Capital formulated by J. S. Mill, and afterwards abandoned in its most essential feature by its author. In spite of the general acceptance accorded to the new position by several important continental economists, they stubbornly refuse to re-open what they have chosen to regard as a dead controversy.

It is hoped that this restatement of the position, by its specific application to the concrete problem of the "unemployed" and by the central importance assigned to the idea of Under-consumption, may avoid some of the misunderstanding to which earlier statements were liable. By its explanation of Unemployment as a natural and necessary result of a mal-distribution of consuming-power, vested in economic rent and monopoly elements of profit, the argument claims a distinct place in the theory of social progress.

The latter half of the book is an endeavour to discover and apply true principles of remedial treatment, by marking the outlines of the larger economic policy which shall embody the principle of progressive consumption, and by the application of a scientific test to the several popular remedies or palliatives which occupy the public attention.

CONTENTS

CHAPTER I

THE MEANING OF "UNEMPLOYMENT"

CHAPTER II

THE MEASURE OF UNEMPLOYMENT

CHAPTER III

DOES UNEMPLOYMENT GROW?

CHAPTER IV

MINOR CAUSES OF UNEMPLOYMENT

CHAPTER V

THE ROOT CAUSE OF UNEMPLOYMENT

CHAPTER VI

THE ECONOMIC REMEDY

CHAPTER VII

BIMETALLISM AND TRADE DEPRESSION

CHAPTER VIII

PALLIATIVES OF UNEMPLOYMENT

THE PROBLEM OF THE UNEMPLOYED

CHAPTER I

THE MEANING OF "UNEMPLOYMENT"

§ 1. *Unemployment as Waste of Labour-Power*

"UNEMPLOYMENT" is perhaps the most illusive term which confronts the student of modern industrial society. This illusiveness exposes the subject to grave abuses. Well-meaning but somewhat hasty social reformers stretch the term and bloat it out to gigantic proportions; professional economists and statisticians, provoked by this unwarranted exaggeration, are tempted to a corresponding excess of extenuation, and are almost driven to deny the reality of any "unemployed" question, over and above that of the mere temporary leakages and displacements due to the character of certain trades, and to the changes of industrial methods.

In order to get some clear understanding of the nature and size of the industrial malady of unemployment, we must, I think, set aside for the present the personal aspects of the subject which appeal most powerfully to human interest, and try to relate "unemployment" to waste of labour-power regarded from the social point of view. This method has the advantage of strict accord with the position held by Mr. Charles Booth, who urges that "the total number of the superfluous is the true measure of the unemployed."

Let us first try to ascertain how far the various classes of those who at any given time would be found to be "off work" can be reckoned as "superfluous" or as waste of labour-power.

Many workers, especially in employments which severely tax the muscular energy, prefer at times to earn their weekly wages by hard labour during four or five days in the week rather than spread their energy more evenly over the six days. This voluntary "play" of the miner or the gas-stoker clearly cannot rank as "unemployment", nor does it, if confined within reasonable limits, involve any waste of labour-power. On the other hand, when "short time" is either forced upon employees, or accepted by them as an alternative to a reduction in the number of employed, such off-time will rightly rank as "unemployment", and implies waste of labour-power.

§ 2. Leakage in "Season" Trades.

Season trades with short engagements usually involve a certain "leakage," as in the intervals between "jobs" in the building trades. A census of "unemployed," taken on a given day, would be apt to include a certain number of masons, bricklayers, etc., who were at leisure for this reason. Yet, so far as this leakage belongs to an irregularity inherent in the trade, it cannot rank as "waste", nor could the labour thus temporarily displaced be regarded as "superfluous." But a strict limit must be assigned to this "necessary" leakage. If the building trade is slack, not only will a smaller number of workers be employed, but the intervals between jobs will be longer. Here there exists a genuine waste of labour-power, which would rightly rank as unemployment. A period of brisk trade in which intervals are smallest must be taken as the right measure of necessary leakage, and even then, if the leakage is due to inadequate organisation in the trade, it implies some waste. In various trades improved intelligence, cheaper travelling, travelling benefits of trade unions, have reduced what would formerly have been considered "necessary" leakage due to natural conditions of the trade.

§ 3. *Is Winter Slackness Unemployment? Official View.*

How far can this view of necessary leakage be extended to the longer intervals of leisure in the building trades and other trades whose irregularity is due to natural causes? The recent Report of the Labour Department upon the Unemployed is disposed to rule out all "unemployment" in the building trades in the winter months.

"A certain amount of time will be lost almost every year during frost. Are the men thus thrown out of work really 'unemployed'? The loss of time may be considered as one of the ordinary trade risks; it recurs more or less every year; it may be supposed to be discounted in the rates of pay earned by members of these trades when fully at work. The bricklayers idle during frost are in no sense 'superfluous,' if the whole year be taken as a unit; were they emigrated or planted in farm colonies, or otherwise lifted permanently off the labour-market, the building trades would presently suffer from a deficiency of men. Nor are they necessarily insufficiently employed. There may be work enough for all, but the trade is such that the work it offers has to be concentrated in certain parts of the year."

This view of compensation forcibly recalls the "economic man" of the old economists, with his infinite capacity for calculating chances, an absolute freedom to select his employment, and a full power to extort from his employer a higher wage to balance any specific disadvantage attending his work. Such a man, being in our present case a bricklayer, might be supposed to obtain such earnings, and so to regulate his expenditure as to hibernate comfortably during the annual period of slackness. The actual bricklayer, though he doubtless can make some provision against the idle season, is not economically strong enough to fully discount in his earnings the irregularity incident to his trade, still less is the bricklayer's labourer able to do so.

If the *a priori* reasoning in the Board of Trade view be accepted, it may be pushed so far as to show that all workers are able to discount all "ordinary trade risks," and to obtain wages adequate to support them during such portion of the year as trade statistics show to represent the average "unemployment" in that trade.

The casual docker, the fur-puller, and all the workers in "season" trades, whose irregularity can be foreseen, ought, according to this theory, to be able to make adequate provision against the "off" period, however long it may be; and since the work of all of them is necessary for the season, their idleness in the off period must not rank as "unemployment", or be regarded as a waste of labour-power.

§ 4. The Social Estimate of " Waste " Labour.

We are not here, however, concerned to discuss how far workers in season trades might or ought to make provision against the times when they are unable to earn wages, but whether the labour-power in such periods is to be reckoned "superfluous" or "waste". Of the literal "superfluity" there can be no question, but is there "waste" from the social point of view? Surely there is. The case is not on all fours with the irregular distribution of work within the week. No true economy of human forces is able to compensate for a winter's idleness by excessive work in the spring and summer months. This "waste" may be due to inherent irregularities of trade, but it is not the less waste. The "unemployment" of the painter during the winter months is not rightly classed with the "leakage" between jobs. In the first place, a good deal of the seasonal unemployment in the building, dock, and many other trades is not necessary or inherent in the nature of the trade, but is attributable to the very existence of a chronic over-supply of labour. If there were not so large a "margin" of labour to make sudden calls upon, the irregularity of many trades would be largely modified. Climatic and other natural causes will doubtless impose a certain amount of irregularity, but a far more regular distribution of employment, even in the building trades, would be possible, if it became necessary; and such readjustment would not imply a waste but ultimately an economy of labour-power, since it would prevent the degradation of *morale* and industrial efficiency which every irregularity of trade produces. Just as in the case of the docks, the recent readjustment of methods of employment has squeezed out and exhibited as "superfluous" a large mass of casual labour which formerly would have ranked as a necessary margin for occasional absorption, so in the building and other trades a similar pressure, modifying methods of work, would expose a like superfluity or "waste" of labour-power. But even if it be held that the distribution of employment throughout the year in these trades cannot be materially altered, it should be admitted that the necessary working of these trades involves a great waste of labour-power by reason of its irregularity. The bricklayers idle during frost clearly represent a superfluity of labour, though not necessarily of bricklaying labour. The, earnest desire expressed by some to provide these season workers with an alternative craft is a virtual admission of the present waste of labour-power.

§ 5. *The " Unemployed" by Trade Depression.*

A very large majority of the skilled workers who are "out of work" at a time like the present owe their unemployment, not to short leakages or seasonal fluctuations, but to great depressions in the manufacturing trade of the country. This, one might imagine, would be at once admitted to imply a superfluity and a waste of labour-power. But the Report on the Unemployed is disposed to think quite otherwise :

"In a period of contraction like the present there are many men who are out of work. They are industrially 'superfluous,' if so short a period as a year be taken as the unit, but over a period of seven years—which for shipbuilding appears to be about the period of the cycle—they are necessary, and were they lifted off the labour-market in slack years there would not be enough men to execute the work when trade revived."

That is to say, when trade is good a large body of men are wanted to work, when trade is bad they are wanted to wait in case it may get better. While they wait their labour-power is not to be considered "waste", because, in the words of Mr. Booth, "our modern system of industry will not work without some unemployed margin, some reserve of labour." "They also serve who only stand and wait," Milton has told us, but this specific application of the truth has seldom been made clear. My chief criticism of the judgment made in the Report is that it begs the entire question with an almost humorous effrontery. As an alternative to the suggestion that without this unhappy margin of "waiters" "there would not be enough men to execute the work when trade revived," I would put the following question: "May not the existence under normal conditions of an average margin of 5 per cent. 'unemployed' in the skilled trades, and possibly a larger margin in the 'unskilled' trades, be a cause, as it is certainly a condition, of the fluctuations which make this year 'good' and that year 'bad'?" If there did not exist this "margin," it is evident trade would not "revive" to the extent it does in such a year as 1889; but, on the other hand, is it not conceivable, that it might not decline so deeply as in 1887? In other words, is it not possible that the fluctuations would be less violent if there did not under normal conditions exist an average "reserve" force of labour to "play

with"? The subject is, of course, far too large for paren-
thetic treatment here, but I cannot forbear to raise this
question in protest against the placid assumption in the
Unemployed Report that there is no "superfluity" of
labour, because the "superfluity," is sometimes for a brief
period mopped up.

· But whatever may be the explanation of trade depression to which we may incline, there can be no question
but that "depression" is directly responsible for a vast
amount of unemployment. Even the Unemployed Report
admits that it would be a "strain of ordinary language
to refuse to these men during slack years the title of
'unemployed'." I further claim that this "unemployment" represents "superfluous," or waste labour-power,
whether the trade depression from which they suffer be
accounted the cause or the effect of the "superfluity."

§ 6. Summary of the Official View of "Unemployment."

If I correctly understand the Unemployed Report,
the only "superfluity" or waste of labour-power which it
admits consists of the following two classes :

"Those members of various trades who are economically superfluous, because there is not enough work in
those trades to furnish a fair amount to all who try to
earn a livelihood at them.

"Those who cannot get work because they are below
the standard of efficiency usual in their trades, or
because their personal defects are such that no one will
employ them."

These classes are represented by a small fringe of
the "skilled" trades who even in fairly good trade fail

to get sufficient employment, and who represent a genuine over-supply of labour-power, and by a large mass of low-skilled inefficient labour of the towns, that superfluous mass which Mr. Booth reckoned in East London to amount to 100,000.

Although the Report confines "superfluity" of labour-power to these narrow limits, the question of "the unemployed" admittedly includes others—viz., all that labour whose temporary displacement is due to changes in methods of industry, changes of fashion, changes in the field of employment, or other causes, which are unforeseen and cannot be reasonably discounted or provided against by the workers.

The Unemployment Report thus narrows down "unemployment" by refusing to include not only "leakages" in employment but seasonal idleness, and it still further limits superfluity or waste of labour-power by excluding the large body of "unemployed" whose condition is due to trade depressions.

§ 7. A Wider Meaning of Unemployed is Legitimate.

I claim to have shown *prima facie* reasons for a wider application of the term "unemployment" than commends itself to the official mind, by the inclusion of all forms of involuntary leisure suffered by the working classes. This connotation has the advantage of being in closest accord with the general usage of "unemployed," and in this sense I shall continue to apply the term. The more scientific definition would, however, identify unemployment with the total quantity of human labour-power not employed in the production of social wealth,

which would rank, under present conditions, as superfluity or waste. This latter, it can be clearly shown, is
not narrower but far wider than the official unemployment.

CHAPTER II

THE MEASURE OF UNEMPLOYMENT

§ 1. *Defective General Statistics.*

EXACT statistical measurement of "the unemployed", or even a close estimate of the total number of those "out of work" at any given time is impossible at present. The miserably defective character of our statistical machinery forms an adequate basis of ignorance upon which to form discreet official answers to awkward questions. But though we cannot directly measure the magnitude of the evil, we are able to show that it is very great.

The only official figure relating to the general quantity of "unemployment" is that percentage calculated by the Board of Trade from the returns furnished to it by trade union officials. The official figure represents the average percentage of members of certain unions who are reported at a given date to be in receipt of unemployed benefit from the union funds. In the December number 1894 of the *Labour Gazette* the figure obtained by averaging the results of sixty-two trade union returns was 7 per cent. But this figure cannot be taken as a general measure of "unemployment." It is not designed as such by the Labour

Department, but is merely quoted as a serviceable index to the general condition of trade and employment in some of our staple manufactures. The Board of Trade exercises no power to compel all trade societies to make returns of "unemployed"; many unions have no record of "unemployed", many that have a record make no return, and many of the returns are too indefinite for use.

§ 2. A Trade Union Average.

But though we cannot take the 7 per cent. average of sixty-two trade unions and apply it generally to the working classes in order to estimate the total of unemployed, we may use it as a serviceable starting-point for legitimate conjecture. In particular, I propose to bring evidence to show how far it is likely that the average of those who are involuntarily "unemployed" is greater or smaller than 7 per cent.

This task requires an answer to three questions:

1. How far can the figure 7 per cent. be taken as a true estimate of "unemployment" among trade unionists?

2. How far would the average "unemployment" among trade unionists be reliable as a measure of unemployment in the whole manufacturing and extractive industry of the country?

3. How will these industries compare with other branches of labour in respect of "unemployment"?

In order to deal effectively with the points involved in the first two questions, it is well to understand how far the sixty-two trade unions which yield the basic 7 per cent. are representative of the general trade of the country. The courtesy of the Labour Commissioner enables me to present the following distribution of the sixty-two unions in relation to the numbers of their members. To these figures I append a third column compiled from the returns of occupations in the last Census Report in order to furnish a general indication as to how far the trade unions in the general groups of industry are fairly representative of the whole body of workers.

Trades.	Number of Unions.	Number of Members of Unions.	Total Occupied in the Trade. *
Engineering and Metal Trades	11	111,889	342,231
Shipbuilding	4	53,895	70,517
Building and furnishing . . .	13	76,043	820,582
Textiles	2	10,629	1,128,589
Mining	2	68,030	561,637
Printing and Kindred Trades	20	34,632	145,307
Clothing, Leather, Glass, etc.	10	4,973	unknown

§ 3. Trades which Contribute to the Board of Trade Returns.

Now the first thing evident is that the trade union figure of unemployment is based on returns which are in many cases too small to adequately represent the mass of industry to which they refer. Only in the case of the

* Employers as well as employed are included here, and, in some cases, a large number of dealers as well as makers. Other difficulties of classification prevent these figures from being anything but a general indication of the relative importance of the several groups of industry.

engineering and metal trades, shipbuilding and printing, can the number of trade unionists, upon whose condition the return is based, be considered large enough to reflect with some degree of accuracy the whole trade to which they belong. In the other cases the condition of certain small sections of a trade or of certain districts can alone be accurately reflected in the returns. These figures are checked and rendered more serviceable in the *Labour Gazette* by the general reports of trades from the several districts. We are thus enabled to see that the large percentage of unemployed is in shipbuilding, engineering and kindred trades. Other information leads us directly or inferentially to the conclusion that the average for the other groups of trade was at the close of 1894 comparatively small, not greatly in excess of what is due to normal trade displacement and personal causes. Indeed, if we take out the shipbuilding and engineering trades, the average of "unemployment" would seem to be so small as to furnish a contradiction to the general idea of slackness and depression which prevailed and which was even reflected in the descriptive reports of the several trades.

§ 4. *No Full Measure of Unemployed Unionists.*

Now it seems to me there is much reason to believe that, so far as the "making" industries are concerned, the figures of "unemployment" furnished to the Board of Trade do not adequately indicate the full measure of "unemployment."

In the first place, it is certain that the number of members returned by the trade union officials as in receipt of unemployed benefit does not fully represent the number of trade unionists out of work. A period of twelve months' membership is commonly required as a qualification for the receipt of unemployed benefit; other conditions are often essential to full membership. Thus a considerable proportion of those included in the aggregate of members are not entitled to receive out-of-work pay, and their unemployment does not appear. For example, only 88 per cent. of iron-founders and only 50 per cent. of shipwrights were eligible for out-of-work pay in 1893 according to the Report on the Unemployed. In most unions "unemployed pay" is only given for a limited number of weeks, seldom extending over thirteen and in some cases for only six; "unemployment" does not generally count as such until a member has been out of work for a week or longer; many are disqualified by falling into arrears in their subscription, a misfortune to which they will be most liable in times of bad trade; some better-to-do workers make it a point of personal pride not to come on their union fund until they are obliged. Owing to these causes, particularly the first, the returns made by the trade unions which only take account of the members who are in actual receipt of "unemployed benefit," gravely under-represent the "unemployment" of trade union members.

Again, the strain of modern competition and the pressure of our great "driving" system bear more and more heavily upon working men who are past their prime of vigour; the age when men are superannuated as no longer able to earn the standard wage is very early in the harder manual trades; and members who are still possessed of a fair measure of efficient labour-power no longer receive "unemployed" benefit, but are placed upon the superannuated or the sick list, receiving aid for a certain period, after which they are left to shift for themselves. Not only among trade union members of skilled trades, but throughout the entire field of industry, the shortness of employment is most largely represented in the progressive under-employment of the middle-aged. In many departments of labour, for example, among miners, sailors, mule-spinners, in metal and machine making, it is practically impossible for a man to have any security of work over the age of forty-five or fifty. Notwithstanding all efforts to retain the appearance of youth, he finds employment slipping from his grasp; his skill and experience avail him little in competition with the younger generation who can outstrip him in pace and muscular activity. In ideal schemes of industrial society it is often held that the twenty or twenty-five years which form the prime of manhood or womanhood afford an ample period for the expenditure of labour-power in the social service. Under present conditions the early compulsory retirement, not into honourable and comfortable leisure, but into a miserable and degrading struggle for the casual means of a bare subsistence, which becomes more precarious as old age advances, must be accounted one of the most terrible forms of the problem of unemployment.

§ 5. Prime Object of Unions to Avoid Unemployment.

In estimating the returns of "unemployed" by the textile, the mining, and other industries, it must be borne in mind that many of the strongly organised trades distribute the loss of employment among all their members, instead of allowing some to become wholly unemployed, working short time instead of allowing a reduction of the number employed. One of the chief objects in the practical programme of many trade unions is the arrangement with employers to work short time so as to avoid unemployment. This, of course, introduces an element of genuine "unemployment" as measured in superfluity or waste of labour-power, which is not returned in the statistics of "unemployed." If all the members of a trade work half time for a period, in any scientific measurement this must reckon at 50 per cent. unemployed. The amount of economic "unemployment" due to this cause is growing all the time as trade organisations become stronger and are able to bring pressure on the employers to distribute a spell of bad trade so as to inflict least injury to the body of workers.

It is then certain that, even among the trade unions whose figures form our basis of calculation, the actual amount of unemployment is greater than is reported.

§ 6. A Larger Figure for Non-unionists.

If we turn to the further question, how far the condition of the trade union is a just indication of the condition of the whole trade, we shall, I think, be driven to conclude that unemployment is greater among non-unionists than among unionists.

In most cases, the members of trade unions must be regarded as the pick of their trade in skill, strength, character and intelligence; and one chief economic object of trade unionism is to secure as far as possible a monopoly of regular well-paid employment for its members, limiting membership by the test of capacity to earn a standard wage. In a period of slack or depressed trade the trade unionist, both by virtue of personal

2

efficiency and by the strength of his union, is more likely to retain employment than the outsider. The less efficient members of a union, whose employment is less secure, fail, in slack times, to keep up their weekly subscriptions, and drop out of the union, whose official report takes no account of them as "unemployed." It is true that against this we must set the ability of the non-unionist to hold his work by a readier acceptance of lower wages. Moreover, as he has no "unemployed benefit" to fall back upon, he will often be driven to take what casual labour of any sort he can get. In measuring the chances of "unemployment," these proba- bilities must be set against the superior position of the union man; but taking the term "unemployed" as com- monly applied to members of a skilled trade, we must without doubt expect to find a larger percentage of "unemployed" among non-unionists than among union members.

§ 7. Unemployed in Unorganised Trades.

Since the unions which effectively maintain out-of-work funds and keep books with sufficient care to be utilised in Board of Trade Reports, are generally the strongest unions, competent to secure for their members the largest share of whatever work is going, the advantage of union- ists compared with non-union members as regards employment will be greatest in those trades. This fact impairs still further the validity of the Board of Trade returns, as indicative of the state of employment in whole trades.

Again, in regarding the trade unions which make returns as a general index of the condition of trade, we cannot fail to observe that the trades which they represent are in most cases the highly skilled and well-organised trades. It is true that some skilled trades are among the most fluctuating, and this is particularly true of shipbuilding, which furnishes so high a percentage of unemployment in the quoted returns. It is sometimes stated that the great fundamental and staple industries which are here represented are more fluctuating in their employment than the minor trades. We have here no means of accurate comparison, but it does not seem reasonable to suppose that this is the case. On the contrary, it seems more than likely that the minor manufactures, which are concerned largely in the supply of luxuries, or at any rate of "unnecessaries", and are subject to innumerable freaks of fashion, or genuine change of natural taste, and which are, moreover, the first to suffer from any depression which affects the spending powers of the community, should on an average present an amount of displacement of labour in excess of that which occurs in the more necessary trades. That this is certainly the case in the present case is, I think, clearly illustrated from the textile trades. The trade union returns refer only to the Lancashire cotton trade. If the minor textile industries in the woollen trade, and particularly in the silk, lace, and linen trades, had been faithfully recorded, a very large quantity of "unemployment" would have been registered.

Between 1881 and 1891 the employment in the lace trade as indicated by the table of occupations in the Census fell off to the extent of 21.3 per cent., the English linens trade fell off 32.3 per cent., while the number engaged in silk and kindred manufactures was diminished by 24.2 per cent. These figures in declining trades do not, it is true, represent the number of those who are at any time unemployed, but they do indicate a large actual displacement of labour.

§ 8. "Skilled" versus "Unskilled" Trades.

Finally, the important question confronts us as to how far "unemployment" is greater in the "unskilled" or "low-skilled" than in the "high-skilled" trades. The *Labour Gazette* 7 per cent. is derived exclusively from the picked members of skilled trades. Is there not a strong presumption that in the low-skilled trades the proportion of economic "unemployment" or waste is much greater?

One result of the organisation of the skilled trades has been to render it more difficult for outsiders to equip themselves for effective competition in a skilled trade. To some extent, at any rate, the skilled unions have limited the labour-market in their trade. The inevitable result of this has been to maintain a continual glut in the low-skilled labour market. This permanent pool of over-supply of low-skilled casual labour is fed by the periodic trade depressions which thrust the weaker members of the skilled trades into the seething mass of low-skilled town workers to struggle for a bare subsistence by irregular labour.

§ 9. Are there Two Questions of "the Unemployed"?

It is sometimes sought to separate entirely the problem of the low-skilled superfluous labour of our towns from the problem of "unemployment" to which skilled workers are subject. But, while the severance may be sound and serviceable in considering modes of relief or remedies, any deeper diagnosis of industrial disorder shows a close organic connection constantly maintained between the two classes of "unemployed". It is true that, in times of good trade, nearly all the members of skilled trades find full employment, while a close investigation among the poorest quarters of our towns would show that even at these times there was a large superabundance of low-skilled, inefficient casual labour. But more minute examination would show that this "sediment" of labour was the gradual accumulation of deposits from the various regular grades of workers, dislodged from their former place in the course of agricultural or manufacturing disturbances, weakened by irregular town life, and breeding weaklings and incapables.

That there does exist, even in periods of normally good trade, a large permanent over-supply of low-skilled and casual labour in all our large towns, there can be no possible doubt. In East London alone Mr. Charles Booth estimated the "waste" or "superfluity" at 100,000 (11¼ per cent. of the whole), not counting therein the lowest dregs of the population:

"It may not be too much to say that if the whole of Class B (100,000) were swept out of existence, all the work they do could be done, together with their own work, by the men, women and children of classes C and D; that all they earn and spend might be earned, and could very easily be spent, by the classes above them; that these classes, and especially class C, would be immensely better off, while no class nor any industry would suffer in the least."

This same class B numbers no less than 317,000 in

the whole of London. The metropolis may be somewhat worse than other cities, but we are brought face to face here with a huge mass of " waste " labour-power which finds no reflection in the reports of the *Labour Gazette.*

Much, if not most, of this low-graded town labour, taken as it is, differs widely in respect of " unemployment" from the case of skilled workers in times of depression. Unemployment here, even more than in the case of skilled workers, becomes a question of " degree." Living by casual and essentially irregular work, few of them could be definitely said to be " out of work " at one time more than another: some scraps of work they must be getting constantly, or they sink into pauperdom. The true measure of unemployment here would clearly be the waste of such labour-power as they possess. This, I take it, is what Mr. Booth meant by his estimate of superfluous labour in East London. Now, if we bear in mind the large mass of our growing town population which is subjected either to the essential irregularities of the low-skilled trades or ekes out a living by casual labour, we shall recognise that even in periods of good trade such a figure as the 7 per cent. which is applicable to skilled trade unionists, would be far below the measure of economic " unemployment" in these classes.

§ 10. Evidence of the Labour Bureaux.

This view of the higher rate of " unemployment" among low-skilled and casual workers seems to be borne out by such direct evidence as is available from the reports of the Labour Bureaux in London, Liverpool, Salford, and other places. Among male applicants for work, general labourers form by far the largest class, while clerks and warehousemen, porters and messengers, contribute a very large proportion of the whole, and far outweigh the members of skilled trades, which are chiefly represented by the building, engineering, and metal trades. Similarly, among ·female applicants for work, charwomen and other general workers have a large predominance. Although no close statistical conclusions as to distribution of unemployment can be drawn from such sources, because the greater helplessness of low-paid labour would more readily drive it to have recourse to these Labour Bureaux, the evidence does warrant us in concluding that "unemployment" is greater among the low-skilled and casual than among the high-skilled labourers.

§ 11. Summary of " Waste" in " Making" Industries.

Following this line of argument, we shall conclude that the 7 per cent. which was taken as our starting-point, is not a full measure of the "unemployment" in trade unions of skilled trades, still less is it a measure of the "unemployment" or the waste labour in the whole body of these trades, and that when we turn from the skilled trades to the less skilled, and from them to the casual labour of our towns, we shall expect to find a far higher average rate of economic waste or "unemployment." If to this we add the inevitable tendency of modern industrial forces, attested plainly by statistics of occupations, to assign an ever-diminishing proportion of national employment to the great staple manufactures engaged in supplying common "routine" wants, and an ever-increasing proportion to subsidiary and luxury trades, which are in their nature prone to irregularity, we shall find good reason to believe that the "waste" of labour-power and the economic "unemployment" in the extractive and manufacturing trades taken as a whole is very much under-represented by the evidence which is drawn exclusively from the higher grades of the best organised trades.

But it must be remembered that our enquiry has so far confined itself almost entirely to the wage-earners in the manufacturing trades and in mining. How far can the conclusions which apply there be extended to employment in general?

§ 12. Proportion of Manufacturing to Distributive Work in England.

We are so accustomed to regard ourselves as a manufacturing nation as to forget that less than one-third of the occupied classes of the English nation are engaged in manufacture. Unfortunately, the method of our Census Returns does not enable us to say with any precision how many persons are engaged in manufactures as wage-earners; but the careful investigations of Mr. Booth into the Census Returns lead to the conclusion that the proportion of English people engaged, not merely in the staple manufactures but in manufactures as a whole, has been gradually declining since 1861. The percentages up to 1881 run as follows:

1841	. . . . 27.1 per cent.
1851	. . . . 32.7 „
1861	. . . . 33.0 „
1871	. . . . 31.6 „
1881	. . . . 30.7 „

If we could separate the "makers" from the "dealers" in our latest Census Report, I feel sure we should find that the proportion of our people engaged in manufactures could not be placed higher than 30 per cent. Taking into account the two great branches of "extractive" industry, agriculture and mining, the recent increase in the latter as regards employment is approximately balanced by the decline of the former. A considerable majority of the "employed" classes, alike in England and in the United Kingdom, are engaged in occupations which we have not yet placed under survey for the purpose of estimating "unemployment" or "waste." An ever larger proportion of our workers and employers are continually engaged in commercial and transport trades and in the various sorts of professional, civil, and domestic service. Now it must be at once admitted that in many large departments of these occupations the quantity of direct "unemployment" and of other labour-waste will be much less than in the manufacturing trades. If, as a rough estimate, we take 13,000,000 as the number of wage-earners in the United Kingdom, it is not likely that more than 4,000,000 * are engaged in manufactures. The large class engaged in retail-dealing, which, from official evidence, seems to be growing more than twice as fast as the population, and which affords an ever-growing proportion of employment, and the "commercial" classes, which in most departments are growing still more rapidly, cannot, I think, be charged with so large a proportion of "unemployment" as belongs to the manufactures.

* The general summary of groups of occupations from the Census of course includes large bodies of employers as well as the whole class of dealers.

§ *13.   Unemployment in Distributive, Transport, and Public Services.*

The chief waste of labour in distribution takes the form, not of "unemployment," but of employment which is excessive and useless from the social standpoint, the multiplication of clerks, warehousemen, shop-assistants, etc., which proceeds far faster than the growth of wares to be distributed. It is true that the evidence of Labour Bureaux shows that large numbers of clerks, shop assistants, and warehousemen are "unemployed", and the heightened competition in these departments of work leads doubtless to an increased precariousness of employment. But in taking a present estimate we should be obliged to assign a lower figure of "unemployment" to commercial than to manufacturing industry. Again, the "transport" industries constantly afford more employment, occupying more than 6½ per cent. of the employed classes. Some large departments of work connected with road-transport show a great "superfluity" of labour, and carmen, stablemen, and others connected with street-traffic figure largely in the lists of the Labour Bureaux: while, apart from absolute "unemployment", there must be an enormous waste of labour-power in cab-driving, etc.

The evidence provided by the registers of Labour Bureaux, though it has a value of its own, must not, I think, be taken as even an approximate test of the proportion of unemployed in the several trades of the localities. The preponderance of general labourers and of those belonging to the building trades amongst men, and dressmakers and seamstresses and charwomen amongst women do, I think, rightly indicate a very large excess

of labour-power as well as a great irregularity in its
demand in these trades, but the very large register of
clerks and messengers, warehousemen and porters, I am
disposed rather to impute partly to the fact that such
workers often cannot take the ordinary means of seeking
work by personal application which is open to those
engaged in manufactures and large-scale industries, and
partly to the absence of trade union organisation upon
which most skilled and some unskilled workers rely to
assist them to a place. But though the classes·of road-
transport are evidently subject to great irregularity, against
this must be set the steady and large employment on
railways and in large departments of navigation.

On the contrary dockers and all branches of riverside
labour will yield a very large quantity of "waste." If we
accept Mr. Geoffrey Drage's estimate of the number of
London dock labourers at 22,000 (exclusive of those
who drift in occasionally from other trades), and compare
it with the average of those actually employed on any
given day, which for the year 1894·amounted to 7,006,
we shall perceive that after allowance is made for the
fairly full work of "permanent" hands, the quantity of
unemployment for the mass must be enormous. Much
of this irregularity is inherent in the nature of a trade
so largely dependent on season and on weather, which
yields a difference of about 25 per cent. for the numbers
employed in March and in November, while the daily
fluctuations are much wider. But even if we take the
maximum employed on the busiest day of the year we
shall find it falls short by some thousands of the number
of "dockers", indicating a large net surplus of "unemployed" not wanted even for short emergencies. In other

ports than London work is not quite so irregular and the permanent surplus of "dockers" is probably much less, but in spite of all efforts to organise and regulate dock employment, the total "waste" of labour in this branch of transport trade must be very large.

` On the whole, the workers engaged in "the conveyance of men, goods, and messages" would yield a far lower rate of unemployment than the manufactures. ˀWe must next add in the rapidly growing department of public services, State, county and municipal, together with the semi-public services of gas, water, electricity, etc. These routine services are essentially regular and would yield no appreciable quantity of "unemployment" either in their civil or military departments, unless we include under the latter the lamentable and criminal waste of "labour" represented by the constant flow of soldiers from regular military service into the Army Reserve, which helps to swell the standing host of untrained and low-skilled labour. One other large class of wage-earners requires mention, those engaged in domestic service. The conditions of this work impose a high degree of regularity in employment, and though the multiplication of registry-offices indicates a large constant flow from "place" to "place", which doubtless involves a certain "leakage" of employment, there cannot, if we take the country as a whole, be a large percentage of "unemployment" or direct "waste" in domestic service. I think that the "unemployment" of servants which figures considerably in the accounts of Labour Bureaux, belongs rather to the large-town problem of general low-skilled labour than to the specific conditions of domestic service. Some over-supply, however, in the lower grades, must be admitted.

§ 14. *General Measure of the Problem.*

The conditions of this estimate of "unemployment" among wage-earners forbid us from venturing even upon an approximate figure for the total of unemployment. I am on the whole disposed to think that if it were possible to take an accurate census upon the subject, we should find that the average for our manufactures as a whole was considerably higher than the figures of the Board of Trade Return (applying the term "unemployed" as usually interpreted by trade unions), but that the bulk of other wage-earning occupations would tend to lower the average of "absolute" unemployment. Interpreted more liberally and more logically as "waste of social labour-time," I think that a figure like 7 per cent. must be considered far below the true measure of this waste. In other words, great as is the evil of complete "unemployment", the evil of irregular and insufficient employment is far greater.

Taking a wider survey of this "unemployed" problem from the social standpoint, we cannot fail to see that it by no means exclusively applies to the wage-earners. That all the professions and the higher arts are "overstocked" has long been a commonplace. Turn where you will—to the law, to medicine, engineering, architecture, teaching, to literature and journalism—you find large numbers of men who are only "nominal" members of their calling, still larger numbers who are always underemployed. Neither here nor in the case of manual workers is it a question of competency or qualifications: set what standard of efficiency you will, the number of well-qualified applicants for any fixed employment, how-

ever moderate the salary, indicates that every grade of
the arts and professions is over-supplied.

§ 15. The Upper Class of Unemployed.

In viewing the subject, not from the exclusive standpoint of poverty, but from that of the social economy
of labour-power, two other classes must be taken count
of before we realise the full waste of labour-power. The
first is the class of upper "unemployed", euphemistically
described in the Census Reports as "unoccupied.") In
1891 there were in England and Wales no fewer than
233,446 males between the age of twenty and sixty-five
who were not even nominal members of any trade or
profession. This represents a large mass of adult labour-
power utterly wasted for purposes of social work, subsisted
out of the labour of others and contributing nothing in
return. A large proportion of this class are well-nourished,
capable men, whose idleness injures both themselves and
the society upon which they live. The casual voluntary
work which some of these may undertake cannot be
regarded as a serious contribution to the aggregate of
social work, being amateur in character and commonly
misdirected, since from the economic nature of the case
it is not amenable to social direction and control.

§ 16. Waste of "Pauper" Labour.

The sum of labour-waste is not complete without an
allusion to the lowest class of "unemployed"—the able-
bodied pauper class. There were on January 1 of last
year, in England and Wales alone, 116,478 able-bodied
adult papers. It is true that most of these, regarded
from the working point of view, would be found hope-

lessly inefficient. But a full consideration of their case
would show that this physical, moral, industrial incapacity
is inseparable from the disorder of a society which has
failed to furnish opportunities of educating and utilising
in the social service the labour-power which in some kind
and degree attaches to every human being. This able-.
bodied pauper class cannot be regarded as a wholly separate
problem, out of organic relation to general problems of
industrial and social order. The forces which.are responsible for other forms of "unemployment" are' engaged in
depositing and maintaining at the bottom of society the
sediment of pauperism. The able-bodied pauper represents
so much potential labour-power which is wasted now.

APPENDIX A.

Unemployment in Registers of Labour Bureaux.

The following statistics, furnished by the Labour Bureaux
established by private philanthropy in nine places, yield
some information as to the occupations of the unemployed during 1894. It must, however, be borne in mind
that five of the nine registers are in cities (London,
Liverpool, Salford, Plymouth, Ipswich) and that four of
them are in the Metropolis (Chelsea, St. Pancras, Batter-
sea, Islington), so that the results bear only upon the
unemployed problem in large centres of population. Moreover, the absolute numbers on the registers are too small
to furnish any close indication of the proportion of unemployment in the several trades, while the number of

Occupations.	Jan.	Feb.	Mar.	Apr.	May.	June.	July.	Aug.	Sep.	Oct.	Nov.	Dec.
Men.												
Building Trades	524	394	265	208	265	264	218	181	212	298	357	325
Engineering and Metal Trades	168	203	182	151	112	149	161	167	170	143	159	148
Woodwork and Furniture	114	79	64	27	18	25	61	69	55	58	52	37
Printing and Bookbinding	45	42	28	22	14	18	23	15	18	18	26	12
Clothing Trades	28	11	20	6	8	10	7	17	16	15	—	1
Carmen,Stablemen,Horsemen&c	256	333	302	239	240	207	262	283	248	245	264	232
Clerks and Warehousemen	125	158	161	108	120	91	116	140	131	103	117	104
Porters and Messengers	310	280	283	204	224	168	195	205	239	261	211	207
General Labourers	537	1,123	819	743	535	541	510	550	496	795	863	777
Other Occupations	179	227	241	213	241	220	179	171	205	176	261	235
Total Men	2,286	2,850	2,365	1,921	1,777	1,693	1,732	1,798	1,790	2,112	2,310	2,078
Lads and Boys	227	234	272	255	249	206	217	217	247	160	139	97
Women and Girls.												
Laundresses	4	5	4	2	—	5	7	1	2	2	2	1
Dressmakers and Seamstresses	33	25	9	7	17	15	10	22	18	13	21	11
Charwomen, daily work, &c..	186	111	146	114	127	153	151	134	124	142	175	124
Servants	113	80	60	48	46	36	76	84	68	46	35	24
Others	23	52	42	17	20	19	11	14	13	15	22	2
Total Women and Girls	359	276	261	188	210	228	255	255	225	218	255	162
Grand Total	2,872	3,360	2,898	2,364	2,236	2,127	2,204	2,270	2,262	2,490	2,704	2,337

centres from which the figures are drawn are not enough to prevent the effects of one or two special local disturbances of industry from exercising an undue influence upon the results, considered as indicative of general conditions of trade.

The totals seem to conform very closely to the general law that employment is better in the summer than in the winter months in the case of men. The statistic of women are so slight and irregular as to have little value.

It will be observed that the building trades and general labourers furnish nearly half the total of unemployed men, but that they are closely followed by the town "transport" trades: carmen, stablemen, horsemen porters and messengers forming a significant feature in the list. The figures, however, considered as representative of the "unemployed," in the several trades, are vitiated by various considerations. Members of skilled trades would seldom place themselves upon the Bureaux registers, preferring to seek work through their business or by personal application at known quarters. Many skilled workmen, clerks and others, would not care to publicly register themselves as unemployed. Charwomen and other day workers will often use the Labour Bureaux as a means of enlarging their connection, misrepresenting the extent of their "unemployment" for this purpose. The workers in irregular trades of the home or small workshop will rarely know the existence of Labour Bureaux. This will possibly account for the small number of men and women belonging to the clothing trades who appear on the registers. Knowledge or ignorance of the existence, purpose, or value of the Labour Bureaux, willingness or unwillingness to publicly acknowledge them-

3

selves as unemployed, existence of other facilities for obtaining work, probability of effectual aid from the Bureaux—these are only a few of the "factors" which determine the register and which render it of small account in its present condition as an index of the distribution of "unemployment" among different classes of industry.

CHAPTER III

DOES UNEMPLOYMENT GROW?

§ 1. Do Modern Forces Make for Irregular Employment?

Is this waste of labour-power arising from chronic insufficiency or from irregularity of employment tending to increase? The question is often put and answered in the affirmative or negative with equal confidence. As we possess no just measure of present "unemployment," and no measure at all of past "unemployment," no direct evidence can decide the point. There are, however, some considerations derived from knowledge of the changes in the character of different industries and the proportion of those employed in these several industries, which will lead us to believe that the general condition of employment in England is one of greater irregularity, and that the waste of time and energy is larger than it was half a century ago or during the 18th century.

§ 2. Expansion of Market Areas.

Three conditions are specially calculated to impress irregularity of employment upon a business. First the wideness of area of the market to the supply of which it contributes. When a manufacturer or a trader supplied a small local market of known customers whose habits of consumption were pretty fixed, and who were practically unable to go for their supply outside this small market, a regularity of local demand prevailed which also implied a regularity of production. The resources and methods of production of one's trade competitors were known and were not subject to such rapid changes as would enable them to draw away quickly a "custom" once established. The expansion of market area, directly attributable to improved methods of communication and transport, renders every business man liable to the keen competition of rivals in distant parts of the country or in foreign lands with whose existence, economic resources, and methods of production he is not familiar. Although he does his best to keep himself *au courant* with the movements of the wider market, that market is constantly growing larger and more complex, and he finds it quite impossible to obtain a knowledge of the corn or wool or iron market of the world so reliable as that which he once possessed of the narrower area. To take a familiar example, the education of the English farmer is utterly inadequate to enable him to follow the world-market for wheat or pigs, which is constantly expanding or contracting by the influence of economic and political factors which are utterly outside his ken. This applies more or less to an ever-increasing number of trades.

§ 3. The Speculative Nature of Modern Industry.

Not only are the individual businesses compelled to

compete with a larger number of unknown competitors in a market with a wider space-area, but a corresponding expansion is taking place in the time-area. Manufacture is less and less to supply present known wants, more and more to provide against future expected wants, and to assist in those auxiliary branches of the machinery of capitalist production which are always becoming more and more complex. A less and less proportion of work is done to supply definite orders, more and more is done for the chance of an unknown sale. In other words a larger proportion of trade is taking on the character of "speculation." Miscalculation and misdirection of industrial energy belong essentially to speculative trade and impress irregularity on employment.

In dealing directly with causes of unemployment we shall see how closely this irregularity is connected with the application of modern machinery and power. Although the co-operation. of large fixed capital in plant and machinery in itself tends to enforce continuity of work upon each business, since the loss incurred by stoppage or contraction is greater the individual finds that the matter is less and less dependent upon his own will and energy, and more and more upon the wider trade forces beyond his control, which, operating by upward and downward pressure of prices, oblige him to an oscillating policy of expansion and contraction which involves a waste in the use of capital and labour.

§ 4. Influence of Taste and Fashion.

The increased influence of taste and fashion makes in the same direction. A larger proportion of labour is constantly engaged in the production and distribution of comforts and luxuries which are more amenable to the caprices of the consumer or of the dealers who are responsible for changes in fashion. The silk trade has always been more irregular in its prices and its employment than the cotton or the woollen trades, and that irregularity is increasing as the refinement and rapidity of fashion-changes obtain a hold over a larger proportion of the consuming public. Formerly there was a constant and fairly steady demand for certain kinds of silk ribbon which it was safe to make " to stock," now changes of fashion spread so rapidly and reach so quickly the mass of the consumers that it is no longer possible to make to stock. The same holds generally of articles of convenience or luxury. These rapid changes of taste can of course only find satisfaction on the assumption that there either exists a great surplusage of productive power which only obtains full use at certain periods and is kept in abeyance at other times, or that the transferability of capital and labour is so great as to enable production to follow the changes of consumption without any considerable waste. No one acquainted with trade will assert the validity of this latter supposition. It follows thus that with the increased control of taste and fashion over industry and the increased adaptability of industry to this control which arises from the great expansion of productive power, irregularity of employment tends to grow.

§ 5. *Transferability of Labour.—General versus Special Ability.*

It is sometimes held that any increased irregularity of employment thus caused is more than compensated by the greater facilities which labour possesses for transferring itself from one place to another place, and from one trade to another trade.

So far as the transferability from one locality to another is concerned, the same causes which have expanded the area of the market for most commodities have certainly expanded the labour-market. A man who is thrown out of work by some local decline of trade is more easily and more quickly able to find an opening in the same trade in another place than was once the case, but I do not believe that this increased fluidity of labour has kept pace with the increased fluidity of general trade. Adam Smith's dictum still holds good that "a man is of all sorts of luggage the most difficult to be transported."

The increased ability of the modern worker who is displaced from one trade to find employment in another trade is frequently asserted by economists. The tendency is, it is maintained, to substitute "general" ability for special manual skill. Formerly a handicrafts-man spent many years in getting a particular form of manual dexterity, and, if he were obliged to find some other occupation, he would have to acquire a new skill in the same slow fashion, besides being limited in his new choice by the specialisation of powers which had warped his general development. Nowadays, it is said, a man, engaged in some particular process, who is displaced can learn in a few weeks or months another process in another trade, or can find in another trade a species of work analogous to that upon which he was formerly engaged. The broad question whether there exists for the average workman to-day an increased transferability of his labour-power depends for its answer upon two sets of considerations. The first has reference to the structure of trades.

§ 6. *Does Division of Labour give Security of Employment in Manufacture?*

In modern manufacturing industry the labour of employees must be roughly divided into three classes, (1) general labour in the care of machinery and superintendence of labour, including the work of overseers, of foremen, and of engineers and smiths who are responsible for the right working of machinery and for repairs; (2) machine-tending specialised to work with some particular machine employed in a single process; (3) highly-skilled work in a special process by handicraftsmen or by those who direct and control a special machine.

When the increased transferability of labour is asserted the first class and a portion of the third class are taken into account. It is evident that the work of superintending labour is mostly of a "general" character and can be transferred without much loss from one trade to another. So, too, the engines and general machinery for producing power, and some of the machinery for transmitting it to specific machines are similar in many industries; so that a good deal of labour in the engineering and in the machine and tool making trades will be transferable. A man who looks after engines in a cotton-spinning mill can find employment in any other kind of mill which uses similar engines. A smith, or a carpenter, or a fitter can adapt himself to a good many different trades. It is obvious that many trades have some "common" foundational character, and that workers engaged upon such work have great transferability. Again in the metal or the textile trades there will be certain special skilled processes, which, since they deal with similar properties of similar - material, will be analogous. The passage of weavers from the woollen mills of Yorkshire to the cotton mills of Lancashire has been not uncommon; watchmakers in Coventry have adapted themselves to the less refined processes of the bicycle trade, while this last has also drawn indiscriminately from the Birmingham metal trades those who could easily adapt themselves to the new work. But when writers dwell with enthusiasm upon these signs of "despecialisation" of labour, as proving the increasing importance of general over special attainments and of bringing an increased freedom and choice of occupation to the workers, they fail to take account of two counter-acting forces. Along with this "despecialisation" and more general in its operation is the constant and finer sub-division of labour, among the great mass of subordinate workers. The machine-tender, the typical modern worker, is constantly being narrowed in his work; the "general" mechanic in the building trades has disappeared, the elaborate and many-sided work of the "plumber" has been so specialised and taken over by machinery that he is now nothing but a "fitter." This subdivision, this "specialisation" is surely the main stream of tendency of which the other is only a counter-acting current of inferior power. Those who speak of the increased importance of "general" as opposed to special capacities in the modern worker deceive themselves, if they think, as they appear to do, that the fact implies greater economic freedom. The modern workman is not "despecialised"; on the average he is more highly "specialised" but. he is less deeply set in his special groove and therefore loses less if he is taken out of it. It is not so much that his work nowadays calls for a

larger absolute amount of general ability but that it calls
for a smaller quantity of special skill. General ability is
only relatively more important in the modern mechanic
and machine-worker.

§ 7. *Transferability of Labour in Other Industries.*

If we turn from manufacture to the extractive industries
concerned directly with getting the raw materials of food
or manufacture, we shall not find any net increase of
ability to transfer labour-power, except from one locality
to another. The Scotch or the Durham coalminer may
try his luck in Pennsylvania, or the Cornish tin miner
may migrate to South Africa, but the saying "once a
miner always a miner" still holds good, and there is
every reason to believe that a miner is more narrowly
specialised and that in the modern strain of competition
a thin-seam "hewer" has less chance than formerly of
working advantageously in a thick-seam mine.

The young agricultural labourer no doubt has more
freedom of choice and can take up town work or work
on the line, but when he is once inured to agricultural
work he can no more quit it for factory or other town
work than can the sailor, the soldier, or the fisherman.
The various departments of the transport and the distributive trades do unquestionably contain a large amount
of labour which is more transferable. Though much
railway labour and some dock labour, as for example the
work of many of the stevedores, is highly skilled, the
bulk of it, together with the work of draymen, messengers,
and the like, rests for its value upon certain common
qualities of muscular vigour and intelligence which can
be diverted without much loss to another branch of the

transport services. A railway-porter, a warehouseman, a man accustomed to drive and to care for horses, has a large and I think an ever larger range of employments open for him.

In mercantile and retail industry the writing clerk and the shop assistant are serviceable by reason of certain capacities of quick perception, accuracy, and address which belong to trade in general rather than to any specific trade. The increased proportion of the labour of the community which is engaged in distribution and in transport tends here to assign more importance to the common as distinguished from the special elements of labour power. But there is some reason to believe that as machinery obtains larger control over those branches of industry, the subdivision of labour which prevails in manufacture will find its way there also, reducing the extent of the present transferability of labour.

The labour of the railway worker and of the "sailor" on a steamship is more specialised than the work of the coachman and the sailor on a sailing-vessel which they have displaced. We therefore cannot look with confidence to the operation of new economic forces to secure greater regularity of work by means of improved transferability of labour.

§ 8. Can the Displaced Worker Take up Another Trade?

Even if it be admitted that a special process in modern industry (especially in manufacture) does not generally require so much time and energy to acquire as formerly, and that a man can thus more easily give up one special work and fit himself for another, it by no means follows

that he can get that other work. It is here that we strike
that second false assumption of those who maintain a
general increase of transferability of labour. Suppose the
structure of modern industry did favour transferability
from one trade to another, the transfer can only be
effective provided the demand for labour in these other
trades gives openings to outsiders. Individuals endowed
with special energy and enterprise are no doubt often
able to turn their hand to another trade, but the average
man, though he could take up some other skilled trade,
if he had the chance, finds that he does not get the chance.
Trade Unions from the practical standpoint see, what
the theoretic economist often refuses to see, that generally
throughout the field of industry the supply of labour,
skilled as well as unskilled, is normally in excess of the
demand, and, acting in their own interests, rightly
direct their energies to making it difficult for an outsider
to compete for their kind of work. As the organisation
of labour grows stronger this policy will be enforced more
rigidly, and that transfer of labour from one trade or
process to another which the structure of industry might
permit, will be prevented by the operation of other social
forces.

Taking a general view of the situation we are driven
to the conclusion that the alleged greater transferability
of labour is not adequate to counteract the forces which
make for irregularity of employment and displacement of
labour. Since a larger proportion of the total number of
employed are coming under the new conditions of industrial life, the absolute quantity of "unemployment" at
any given time due to these causes must be increasing.

CHAPTER IV

MINOR CAUSES OF UNEMPLOYMENT

§ 1. The Individual Moral View of the Problem.

In order to realise the relative importance of the economic causes which are directly responsible for "unemployment," some deductions from our earlier analysis may be of service. The common notion of the "philanthropist" and the moralist who, wholly untrained in economic thought, thinks the only thorough treatment of this and other problems of poverty consists in the treatment of individual character, need not detain us long. The fallacy is one necessary to all individualist views of society. A depression of the staple trade in a town throws out of employment 10 per cent. of those who are normally employed. The charity organiser with his individual scrutiny sets to work, and a close investigation of each "case" discloses in most of this 10 per cent. some moral or economic defect: there is drink, laziness, inefficiency, or some other personal fault discernible in, or imputed to, most of these "unemployed." Our "thorough" investigator, having, as he thinks, found a sufficient reason why each man should be unemployed, reaches the conclusion, that "unemployment" is due to individual causes. Such conclusion is, of course, wholly fallacious. Personal causes, no doubt, explain in a large measure who are the individuals that shall represent the 10 per cent. "unemployed", but they are in no true sense even contributory causes of the "unemployment." When economic causes lower the demand for labour, competition will tend to squeeze out of employment those individuals who, for reasons, sometimes moral, sometimes industrial, are less valuable workers than their fellows. If these individuals had not been morally or industrially defective they would have kept their work, but necessarily by pushing out other 10 per cent. Personal causes do not to any appreciable extent cause unemployment, but largely determine who shall be unemployed. The individualist-moralist is keen to detect the fallacy involved in supposing that poverty can be stopped by regarding it as a number of holes to be filled up by pouring in promiscuous charity. But he does not perceive that this analysis and treatment of "unemployment" involves a fallacy closely analogous to that which he has condemned.

§ 2. *Nature of the Individualist Fallacy.—Character Determining Who Shall be Unemployed.*

The moral and industrial elevation of defective individuals is, for their individual sakes and on general moral grounds, highly desirable, but it will have no *direct* effect in diminishing unemployment.

This may appear to some a hard saying. But it is strictly true. The effect of the McKinley tariff in causing depression of trade and unemployment in Bradford is not really dependent upon the moral or industrial qualities of those workers who are displaced. If these latter, who will be found less efficient or less reliable on the average than those whose services were retained during the depression, could be morally and technically educated above the level of their fellows, this fact would not prevent the same external forces from operating upon Bradford with the same effect as before. Different individuals might be displaced from employment, that is all. A sudden fall of the fashion for wearing silk ribbons will reduce the employment of Coventry weavers, and no moral or industrial elevation of the workers will affect the quantity of unemplyoment which is caused. Even if it be allowed that a rise of the average efficiency of the Bradford or Coventry workers would enable them to keep some of their trade by underselling the competitors in other towns or other countries in a time of depressed trade, they would only escape unemployment by throwing out of work their weaker competitors in other places: the trade as a whole would suffer just as much from unemployment as before. The notion that an increase of productive power will be a safeguard against employment will not stand for one moment when confronted with the fact, that during each period of unemployment a large existing excess of productive power is the most striking phenomenon.

Indirectly there is no doubt that all forces which contribute to the intellectual and moral education of the workers help to maintain employment in so far as they stimulate a demand for a higher standard of life, which will find expression in an increased effective demand for commodities.

But this does not justify us in stating that moral or technical inefficiency are considerable causes of unemployment in face of the fact that during periods of ordinarily good trade most of those very individuals whose " unemployment" is imputed to " personal defects" are found to be in regular

work, or in supposing that moral and technical education
will help directly either to prevent or cure unemployment.

It is perhaps almost inevitable that those who are
absorbed in work amongst the poor should often be dupes
of this individualist fallacy. Personal defects commonly
appear as direct and sufficient reasons why A or B or
C fail to get regular work, and if Society at large is
regarded merely as a conglomerate of particular instances
of A and B and C, these personal defects appear to
furnish a sufficient explanation of the total amount of
poverty or of unemployment in the whole society. But
this conclusion, very natural to those immersed in detailed
cases, and unable to see the forest for the trees, ignores
utterly the interrelations of the various individuals and
the organic unity which they express. Regarded as furnishing an explanation of "unemployment," it rests upon a
total denial of the operation of wider economic forces
determining the quantity of employment available at a
given time for a working community. If it is true, as
all students of economics assert, that there are forces
operating from without which are liable to cause a shrink-
age of employment in the woollen or the iron trade,
amounting to (say) 30 per cent. of the former volume of
employment, it is idle for those who, working as philanthropists, shut their eyes to these economic forces, to
adduce as causes of "the unemployment" those personal
causes which merely decide whether A or B or C among
the workers shall be among the 30 per cent. unemployed.

It has been necessary to emphasise this point because
the grasp of an organic conception of industrial life and its
necessary implications is still very weak, and the notion
that investigation which confines itself to particular instances

alone contributes a thorough and a scientific treatment is very prevalent among many of those who claim to speak with authority on the questions of poverty and unemployment.

§ 3. *Connection of Machinery with Unemployment.*

It can, I think, be clearly shown that the great mass of "unemployment" and "under-employment" is not due to those "minor" leakages which belong to the character of certain trades or even to the detailed changes of machinery, industrial method, and *locale* of markets, which we saw were *veræ causæ* in the problem. At certain periods, large sudden displacements have, of course, been attributable to the substitution of machinery for handlabour or to some great political event affecting markets. If, however, we confine ourselves to British trade in recent years we cannot explain by these means the great fluctuations of employment.

It is a mistake to regard as one of the necessary effects of improvements in machinery and their substitution for hand-labour a great mass of unemployment. The introduction of new machinery into a trade must under existing circumstances inflict a twofold injury upon those whose labour it affects. It reduces or destroys the market-value of the special skill they have acquired, and it imposes upon some or all of them the necessity of finding other work, where their special skill is not available. But if the general condition of the labour-market were such that the demand for labour pressed upon the supply, such displaced labour would be rapidly re-absorbed and the total waste by "unemployment" would be very small. In the prosperous period 1871-4 machinery made considerable strides in many English industries, and many "savings" of labour were effected, especially in the metal

4

trades; but the expanding demand for labour was so great that a very small proportion of the working population was at any time out of employment. Where improvements of machinery occur during periods of "booming" trade they do not occasion any large quantity of unemployment or distress. It cannot therefore be held that the application of improved machinery, is itself a chief and necessary cause of unemployment.

§ 4. Estimate of Minor Causes. Trade Depression shown as Major Cause.

These machinery changes and specific trade movements are, of course, extremely numerous and of continual occurrence. For this very reason, in taking a term of years their influence may be discounted. The amount of "unemployment" due to these causes must be taken as a pretty constant quantity. A glance at the statistics of unemployment recorded by the Board of Trade during the last nine years will indicate the importance of this conclusion.

At End of each Month.	1887	1888	1889	1890	1891	1892	1893	1894	1895
January	10.3	7.8	3.1	1.4	3.4	5.0	10.0	7.0	8.2
February ...	8.5	7.0	2.8	1.4	2.6	5.7	9.5	5.6	7.9
March	7.7	5.7	2.2	1.7	2.8	5.7	8.7	6.5	6.5
April	6.8	5.2	2.0	2.0	2.7	5.4	6.9	6.1	6.3
May	8.5	4.8	2.8	2.0	3.8	5.9	6.2	6.3	6.0
June	8.0	4.6	1.8	1.8	2.9	5.2	5.8	6.3	5.6
July	8.5	3.9	1.7	2.3	3.3	5.0	6.2	7.4	5.3
August	8.3	4.8	2.5	2.3	4.2	5.1	7.1	7.7	5.2
September ..	7.5	4.4	2.1	2.6	4.5	6.2	7.3	7.6	4.9
October	8.6	4.4	1.8	2.5	4.4	7.3	7.3	7.4	4.9
November ..	8.5	3.1	1.5	2.4	3.8	8.3	7.2	7.0	4.3
December...	6.9	3.3	1.7	3.0	4.4	10.2	7.9	7.7	4.8

§ 5. *Short Period and Long Period Fluctuations.*

Now, if in the skilled trades here represented we are justified in counting the minor "leakages" and special displacement due to introduction of new machinery, etc., as a fairly constant quantity, taking one year with another, we cannot fail to recognise that some greater forces are at work which account for the large bulk of the unemployment here displayed. In January, 1890, the necessary minor "leakages" and specific displacements were going on, and yet these only caused 1.4 unemployment. If, then, we are called upon to explain why in January, 1887, 10.3 men are "unemployed," we must seek another cause or causes. A further comparison of one year as a whole with another will disclose the fact that the force to which we must attribute the mass of unemployment is one which operates over wider periods than a year. We are driven irresistibly to the conclusion that the great tidal movements of trade, and not the minor detailed movements of special trades, are the root-causes of the evil we are investigating. No accumulation of minor short-period causes will explain why, on the average, throughout 1889 the rate of "employment" was only 2.1, while in 1887 it was 8.1, and in 1893, 7.5.

So far as these statistics of skilled trades can be taken as an index of general trade movements, we must conclude that the great trade depressions are the vital factor with which we have to deal, and that no palliatives or cures will be of much service unless they serve to mitigate the force of these vast world-movements in trade.

§ 6. *Strikes as Causes of Unemployment.*

It is not infrequent for business men and others who have not followed sufficiently closely the periodic fluctuations in prices and volume of trade during the last half century to assign Strikes as the chief cause or as an important contributory cause of bad trade and of unemployment. So it is urged by a writer in the *National Review* * that the high percentage of " unemployment " at the opening of 1893 must be attributed to the " cotton strike ", the suggestion being that all " unemployment " which is not explained by necessary leakage and specific trade displacements is a voluntary suspension of work arising from excessive claims of the workers. " These people rebel against their masters, make extortionate and impossible demands, and after striking work or being locked out assume the role of men unable to get work and wages "—is the frequent comment made by the unthinking members of all classes. Now in the first place there is no close correspondence between the great strikes and a high rate of unemployment : comparatively few strikes of any importance have occurred in the trades whose unions are well-ordered enough to furnish proper statistics to the Board of Trade, or in trades which closely affect them. The coincidence of the cotton strike with the high general percentage of " unemployment " was exceptional. But even were it true that all periods of great unemployment were marked by strikes or by lockouts resulting from action of the workers, we should be quite unjustified in stopping our enquiry at this point.

* Miss. H. Dendy, "Socialistic Propaganda," September 1895.

There is an overwhelming weight of evidence to show that most great strikes are symptoms and results of trade-depressions, not causes. The three large strikes of recent years, those connected with Dock Labour, the Cotton Trade, and Coal Mining, were all of this character. Schulze-Gaevernitz in his careful and impartial investigation of English industry finds the real cause of the great Dock Strike in 1889 in the financial weakness of the Dock Companies, attributable to the fact that "Too many docks had been built and there was the fiercest competition between the Companies." * The persistent fall of prices due to "over-production" is assigned as the explanation of the cotton-strike of 1893. † The cutting down of contract prices under the pressure of the same forces brought about the great lock-out in the Coal-mining industry. Other ostensible causes are sometimes to the front, but most modern strikes are conditioned by an excess of producing power in the several trades, which drives employers to lower prices which they can only render profitable by reducing wages or by introducing new labour-saving machinery or by other economies which directly diminish the demand for labour. The only strikes which we are entitled to count as voluntary unemployment and for which allowance should be made in our analysis of economic causes, are those made for a rise in the standard wage or some other definite improvement in the economic condition of a class of workers, or the rare case of a sympathetic strike. Speaking generally a strike is not a cause but an effect of depressed trade

* "Social Peace," p. 262.
† Cf. De Rousier, "*La Question Ouvrière en Angleterre*," pp. 455—458.

and is preceded by a fall of prices in the goods with the production of which the trade is concerned.

§ 7.   *Unemployed Capital and Land as well as Labour.*

One final statement belongs to an understanding of the nature and magnitude of the disease. " Unemployment " of labour, waste of labour-power, does not stand alone. At the great periods of depression, we have not only "unemployed" labour, but "unemployed" capital. Nor can it be accounted a mal-adjustment of capital and labour as between trade and trade. The special characteristic of industry during a period of trade depression is that, not in this or that trade, but over the general field of industry, there is labour-power and capital lying "unemployed." The actual phenomenon is a general excess of productive power. The waste of labour-power in our modern communities is evidently but one important aspect of an even larger economic problem. This question is one we may well allow to germinate in our minds. "Why is it that, with a wheat-growing area so huge and so productive that in good years whole crops are left to rot in the ground, thousands of English labourers, millions of Russian peasants, cannot get enough bread to eat? Why is it that with so many cotton-mills in Lancashire that they cannot all be kept working for any length of time together, thousands of people in Manchester cannot get a decent shirt to their backs? Why is it that, with a growing glut of mines and miners, myriads of people are shivering for lack of coal?" These questions are not conceived in a spirit of sensationalism, but merely to bring home the nature of the vital problem which is forced more and more upon thinking men and women: "Has our general standard of consumption risen to a degree commensurate with the prodigious increase of productive power brought about by modern improvements in machinery and methods of industry, and vested in modern forms of labour and capital?"

CHAPTER V

THE ROOT-CAUSE OF UNEMPLOYMENT

§ 1. Fallacy of the Piecemeal Treatment of the Unemployed Question.

A MISAPPLIED respect for thoroughness often leads students of society to a piecemeal treatment of industry which blinds them to a perception of large organic operations. It is natural that men of business, whose interests and sympathies are absorbed in some special trade and some special locality, should mistake their knowledge of local symptoms for a thorough diagnosis of industrial disease. But it is not so creditable that statesmen and economists should do their best to make it appear that the "unemployed" is not one, but a hundred different questions to be studied only in detail and to be solved by a hundred different little local remedies. This detailed research is highly necessary, but it can lead us only to a knowledge of secondary and contributory causes; no clear understanding of the problem is attained until this fragmentary knowledge is gathered into the unity of a higher synthesis.

The piecemeal method which commends itself so signally to Royal Commissions upon Labour or Committees upon "The Unemployed" does not really deserve the character it claims of being "thorough." Refusing to investigate the wider operation of economic forces and discarding all "theoretic" considerations, these practical persons confine themselves to collecting elaborate memoranda of minor facts, while ignoring the major facts by which alone they can order and interpret their details When the British mind is driven to take in hand a question like that of "the unemployed" its first instinct is to chop it up into a number of little questions, and again to subdivide these into an infinite number of smaller portions. It then proceeds to collect "evidence" —huge quantities of little local facts and figures which it serves up in crude masses through Blue Books. An attempt is sometimes made to reach minor generalisations bearing upon some detailed aspects of the general question, but no endeavour is made to focus the evidence in any bearing upon the unity of the subject.

§ 2. Need of a Unified Organic Treatment.

All this work of laborious detail is useful, it ought to be done, but not the other left undone. The method is really not scientific but the reverse. It attempts to treat a unified organic subject by a piecemeal inorganic method. Its collections of facts never attempt to go behind concrete phenomena into the wider movements of industrial life, so as to find out what mal-adjustment of the larger economic forces is really represented in unemployment. The notion that scientific thoroughness consists in breaking up an organic whole into a number of inorganic pieces would be simply humorous if it were not fraught with the most injurious effects upon the reputation

of sociological studies. It is not really scientific to specialise without any "fundamentum divisionis", and without
any attempt or intention to apply the results of specialised enquiry to a philosophic interpretation of the subject as a single whole. "There is no Social Problem,
there are only social problems," Gambetta is reported to
have said. This is the attitude of most of our statesmen
and many of our economists: it is the typical position of
the politician and the academic person. Being a practical
denial of the possibility of Social Science, the very existence of which depends on the admission of unity in the
subject matter, the prevalence of this falsehood explains
why progress in social study is so slow. It also explains
the vague and chaotic character of the general judgments
to which our public bodies of enquiry commit themselves
when they occasionally break loose from the tabulation
of raw facts. A delightful example of this judgment is
contained in the Final Report of the Labour Commission,
when that body, confronted with the necessity of saying
something on the wider aspects of Irregularity of Employment, gives vent to the following:

"Fluctuations of trade in this country are due to a
variety of causes, the chief of which may be briefly
indicated here. The majority of these periodical changes
are connected in some way with the state of commercial
credit, and the willingness or unwillingness of business
men to embark on new ventures. The state of credit in
every country depends each year more and more upon
the general conditions of business throughout the world."

Omitting the middle terms of this syllogistic argument, we
attain the valuable conclusion that irregularity of employment
is attributable to "the general conditions of business"!

§ 3. Central Fact—General Excess of Producing Power.

Neither in the proceedings of the Labour Commission nor in the analysis of causes of unemployment contained in the Report of the Board of Trade do we find the faintest recognition of the central fact of the "unemployed" problem—viz., the simultaneous general unemployment of labour, capital, and land in periods of depressed trade. Our analysis of the available statistics forced us to the conclusion that the "unemployed" question was in the main a leading aspect of the problem of trade depression. From the financial point of view bad trade appears as a general lowness of prices and of profits, but, regarded as a disease of the industrial structure, it takes the shape of a general slackness or under-use of the various factors of production. Now, no serious attempt has been made, by what may provisionally be called the orthodox school of English economists, to explain why it is that at one and the same time there can be in existence more labour, more capital, and more land, than are wanted. There might exist, according to their theory, more labour than could be employed, owing to an insufficiency of capital with which to assist labour to produce; but, since capital and labour are the only requisites for the production of wealth, they could not both be in excess. The common mode of meeting the difficulty was to deny the fact of a general excess of producing-power. There might, it was alleged, be an excessive application of capital and labour to certain trades, but this was a malady of mis-direction, general excess of producing-power was impossible.

§ 4. *A Priori Assumptions of Economists.*

This view has always been based upon an *à priori* assumption that whatever is produced can be sold and must be sold because it was produced for no other motive, the validity of which assumption I shall discuss later on. Here it is enough to say that the theory that over-production in some trades implies under-production in others, and that the malady is only the necessary mis-direction of productive energy arising from imperfect acquaintance with markets, is inconsistent with the facts at a time of depressed trade. Where are then to be found the under-producing trades, those which are insufficiently fed with capital and labour, and where, in consequence of the growing inability to satisfy demand, prices are rising? There are no such trades. The fall of prices, the depression of trade, the slack employment are general not special in application. The glut of loanable capital is sufficient proof. If there were trades which were under-producing this free capital would flow into them. A continued glut of loanable capital seeking investment is only consistent with the admission that all avenues of sound investment are already occupied.

§ 5. *True Meaning of " Over-production."*

But when the state is described as one of over-production, a certain misconception often arises. If by over-production is meant a continued process of glutting the markets with goods which cannot find purchasers and are accumulated in ever-increasing quantities, such an operation is not possible. A comparatively small quantity of goods which are " over-produced" in the 'sense that their addition to supply drives prices below the margin of profitable production will suffice to "congest" a trade. If fixed expenses are very heavy, production may be carried on for some time at a loss, but always at a slackened pace, while it is only a question of time when the weaker businesses are driven to suspend operations and the stronger to a close restriction of their output, sometimes accompanied by a trade dispute which checks for a time the whole volume of production. In no trade can actual over-production of goods continue for any long period, though the liability to over-produce may manifest itself in actual gluts from time to time over a long period of years. The true signification of over-production as used to designate the immediate cause of depression is the continued existence of a general excess of producing-power in the forms of capital and labour beyond what is economically required to supply the current or prospective rate of consumption of the community.

§ 6. *Authorities Admit a General Excess.—Evidence of Commission.*

But if what is signified is a long continued existence of a general excess of producing-power beyond what is economically required to supply the current rate of consumption, such excess is plainly attested by modern industry. Moreover, it was admitted in unmistakable language by the same Majority Report of the Commission on the Depression of Trade in 1885, which rejected with scorn the notion of "a general over-production." In its general summary this Report says, "That owing to the nature of the times the demand for our commodities does not increase at the same rate as formerly; that *our capacity for production is consequently in excess of our requirements*, and could be considerably increased at short notice; that this is due partly to the competition of the large amount of capital which is being steadily accumulated in the country." The Minority Report finds the gist of trade depressions in "a long-continued fall of prices—in many cases the result either of actual over-production or of a capacity of production in excess of the demand." This Commission entirely throws over the notion, which every man of wide business experience has long repudiated, that an excess of producing-power in some trades must be balanced by a deficiency in others, and that there can be no general excess. The idea that depressed trade means a mis-application of capital and labour as between trade and trade is entirely rejected by both bodies of Commissioners, who find the malady they are investigating common to all "productive industries." The Minority expressly asserts over-production, in the sense above taken, as the chief agent in depression:

"Over-production, by which we understand the production of commodities (or existence of the agencies of production) in excess, not of the capacity of consumption, if their distribution were gratuitous, but of the demand for export at remunerative prices, and of the amount of income or earnings available for their purchase in the home market—that is, of profitable employment for the people. The depression under which we have so long been suffering is undoubtedly of this nature."

The Majority, though rejecting the general term "over-production," admit, as we saw, the phenomena.

§ 7. The Testimony of Recent Industrial History.

The one fact which emerges with striking clearness
from the whole investigation of the period 1875-1885 is
that the producing-power of capital and labour, to which
full employment was given in the years immediately
following the Franco-German war, was found excessive
in quantity during the ten years which ensued. The
same trade-malady—general under-employment of capital
and labour—has been plainly visible since 1890. In
trade after trade it has been made manifest that the
capacity of production is far in advance of the current
or expected demand at a profitable price, and in all of
them brief bursts of activity have alternated with long
periods of torpor, during which weaker mills, mines and
works are closed, while others are working short time,
and large bodies of workers are kept half-employed. In
three staple industries, docks, cotton, coal-mining, the
attempts to fully utilise existing powers of production
were directly responsible for prolonged stoppages, during
which the congestion was relieved at a terrible cost of
suffering to the workers. A strike or a lock-out, attributable to
a fall of prices, would, as we have seen, rightly rank as so much
"unemployment" in any true economic analysis, though
the immediate cause might be a disagreement between
capital and labour in reference to wages or other terms
of employment. All business men are compelled to admit
that at the present time there exists, not in this industry
or that, but in all the important industries of the country,
a considerably larger quantity of plant and labour than
can be profitably employed. A general consensus of
practical opinion would sustain the judgment recently

affirmed by an experienced business man, "So rapid has been the advance in production, whether agricultural or mechanical, so greatly have the means of transportation and communication improved and cheapened that *supply always now outruns demand.*" * Indirect testimony of the most valuable kind is afforded by Von Halle in his treatment of the American Trust. "Before the establishment of the combinations, hardly any industry had been able to utilise its full capacity. For instance, even before the days of the Cotton Oil Trust, numerous presses and refineries had for a long time been inactive. The Trust closed at once more than a dozen of the small old-fashioned mills. The same thing happened with the Sugar Trust, which can supply the whole market with the product of one fourth of the plant it owns. The Whiskey Trust immediately closed 68 of its 80 distilleries, and with the remaining 12 was enabled to furnish the same output as before and soon to largely increase it." †

In other words, with the means of production which now exist a far larger quantity of commodities could be produced than are actually produced. It is probable that the percentage of unemployed or under-employed capital in the shape of mills, ironworks, dockyards, mines, and plant and machinery of various kinds is far larger than the 8 or 10 per cent. which may represent the waste of labour-power. From the financial point of view the excess is attested by the universal glut of loanable capital to which Mr. A. J. Wilson has recently directed public attention. § Another financial authority, Mr. Van Oss,

* J. H. Trotson, "The Assault on the Standard."
† Von Halle, "Trusts." p. 66.
§ "Investor's Review," January 1895.

rightly associates the glut of money with a glut of capital, affirming that "the amazing production of wealth under the new industrial conditions is rapidly altering the proportion between the supply of capital and the demand for it." *

§ 8. *Failure of Consumption to Keep Pace with Growth of Productive Power.*

The opening up of vast new tracts of land for the growth of our food and raw material of manufacture, the huge accumulation of capital in the shape of fixed plant and power-driven machinery of manufacture and transport, the rapid growth of an intelligent and closely co-operative population have, during the last few generations, multiplied twentyfold or more the general productive power of the community. The actual standard of consumption for nearly every class of the community has likewise been raised. The landowning classes live far more expensively than they did at the opening of the present century; the owners of manufacturing and trading capital form a numerous new class of consumers whose expenditure has grown continuously; statistics of working-class life show that, except among the very poor, the general standard of comfort is considerably higher than it was, though the stability of the standard is grievously impaired by growing irregularity of work. But, great as this general rise in the consumption of the people may .appear, it has been far less rapid than the growth of productive power. The industrial revolution has not been attended by a commensurate revolution in the consuming habits of

* "Nineteenth Century," April 1896.

the people. If modern machinery and methods of production have raised twentyfold the producing-power, the
consumption of the community has increased at a lower
ratio. We therefore find that the several agents of production exist in excess; full and continuous use cannot
be found for them. This is no theory, but a just summary of the phenomena of modern industry. Why such
excess of wealth-producing power is possible may remain
an open question, but of the fact there can be no dispute. It is not a case of improper application of productive power, an excess in certain trades, or at certain times,
balanced by a deficiency in other trades or other times.
It is a normal and general condition of excess. The
rate of production of commodities actually maintained in
the years 1871-4 could have been continued during the
ten years which followed, if the demand had not slackened; and the fact that it was not so continued is a clear
admission of a grave excess of productive power under
normal conditions of national life.

§ 9.   *Wasteful Multiplication of Distributors.*

This excess of general producing-power is far from
being adequately represented by the average unemployment or under-employment of capital and labour in the
extractive and manufacturing industries. " Unemployment "
is only one form of the waste. Another is the socially
useless multiplication of middle-men and other distributors,
and of the capital engaged in distributive businesses.
Unable to find remunerative employment in "productive "
industries, an increasing proportion of capital and labour
is engaged in the work of distribution. This movement
is unmistakably attested by the Statistics of Occupations

in the Census Reports. The common notion that we are
becoming more and more a manufacturing nation is
incorrect so far as employment of labour is concerned.
Taking the aggregate of the manufactures from the Census
returns, as interpreted by Mr. Charles Booth,* it appears
that whereas up to 1861 manufactures engaged an increasing proportion of our population, since that date, although
there continues to be an absolute increase in the numbers
so employed, that increase is slower than the growth of
the population. The percentage engaged in manufactures
from 1841 to 1881 is as follows :

    1841 . . . . 27.1 per cent.
    1851 . . . . 32.7   „
    1861 . . . . 33.0   „
    1871 . . . . 31.6   „
    1881 . . . . 30.7   „

Though we cannot place in exact line with the preced-
ing returns the results for 1891, there is every reason to
believe that the proportionate decline of employment has
continued, and that not more than 30 per cent. of the
occupied classes are engaged in manufactures. Set off the
increase of coal-miners against the decline of agricultural
workers, and an aggregate decline of the numbers engaged
in extractive industries is obtained. What, then, has
become of the one million and three-quarters added to
our working population between 1881 and 1891 ? Outside
the manufacturing and extractive industries there is only
one other large department of "making" industry, the
building trades. But here the employment between 1881
and 1891 only increased by a paltry 2.1 per cent., as
compared with a growth of 15.1 per cent. of the occupied

* "Occupations of the People, 1841—1881."

classes as a whole.   The answer is that the trades engaged
in distribution are growing quite out of proportion to the
growth of the population.   While the agricultural class has
positively declined, the domestic class grown only 5.4 per
cent., the industrial class 15.1 (just keeping pace with the
growth of the occupied population as a whole), the commercial
class shows an increase of 42.8 per cent.   When we turn to
investigate more closely this increase of the commercial
class, we find that "merchants and agents" have grown
in ten years from 285,138 to 363,037, an increase nearly
twice as fast as that of the occupied population.   The
division engaged in wholesale dealing, money and insurance has increased 33.1 per cent.   Bank clerks and officials have increased from 14.998 to 19,975, dealers in
money have grown by 31 per cent., insurance agents
have actually doubled their numbers.   Commercial clerks
and travellers are increasing rapidly, the former 24.2
per cent., the latter no less than 36.2 per cent. in the
decennium.

§ 10.   The Abnormal Growth of Retail-Traders. ·

Owing to the fact that many "dealers" are classed
with "makers" in the Census returns, it is not possible
to make a full and accurate computation of the growth
of those engaged in retail trade.   But the following comparison of those engaged in retail trades where the dealers
are separated from the makers is most instructive :

Trades.	1881	1891	Increase or decrease per cent.
Chemists	19,000	21,930	+ 15.4
Booksellers	9,910	13,596	+ 37.2
Stationers	15,241	21,798	+ 43.0
Drapers	82,362	107,018	+ 29.9
Haberdashers	9,565	12,481	+ 30.5
Grocers	129,818	181,856	+ 40.1
Poulterers and Fishmongers	21,497	29,711	+ 38.2
Greengrocers, Fruiterers. .	29,614	40,963	+ 38.3
Cheesemongers, Buttermen.	4,397	5,108	+ 16.6
Butchers	81,702	98,921	+ 21.1
Coal dealers	20,401	23,799	+ 16.7
Ironmongers	16,122	21,444	+ 33.0
General Shopkeepers . . .	54,860	53,608	− 2.3
Total	494,471	632,233	+ 27.9

§ *11. The Causes of Waste of Distributive Power.*

It thus appears that, in spite of all economies of con-centration resulting from the increased amount of distribution which has fallen to large stores and universal providers, the increase in the number of retail distributors is nearly twice that of the occupied classes as a whole. To put the matter succinctly, a smaller proportion of the population is engaged in "making" the increased quantity of material goods which are consumed, a larger proportion in distributing them. Nor is this movement adequately explained by the fact that distribution has not shared equally with manufacture the economies of modern machinery and method. For the large growth of our population and its concentration in larger towns must have greatly reduced the labour-cost of distributing a given quantity of goods. This consideration, taken along with the improvements in every mode of transport, would enable the increased quantity of modern wealth to be effectively distributed without any considerable increase of the labour or capital engaged in distributive industries. Even if some increase of distributors be economically necessary, it will not be denied that the actual increase of all classes of middle-men and retailers has passed far beyond this wholesome necessary limit. A diminishing proportion of commercial effort is expended in the actual work of distribution, an increasing proportion in the work of getting business. `A proof of this is the phenomenal growth of commercial travellers, local agents, jobbers, touts, and the enormous expenditure in every form of advertisement. The actual energy given out in trades, directly or indirectly concerned in distribution, is thus swollen far beyond the demands of such wholesome and effective competition as will ensure for the consuming public a cheap and rapid service of supply. The keenness of competition among rival distributors is admittedly responsible for much of the adulteration and other deceitful practices which tend to the deterioration of commodities. Unfortunately, we possess no official or reliable records of the general movements in retail trade, which we can compare with the statistics of wholesale prices prepared by Mr. Sauerbeck. It is, however, generally believed, and such fragmentary evidence as we possess accords with the belief, that the great fall of wholesale prices since 1873 has not been attended by a commensurate fall of retail prices.

§ 12.   Why Waste takes a Different Form in Distribution and in Manufactures.

Nor is it unreasonable that this should be the case. The effects of competition are somewhat different in manufacturing and in distributing industries. In the former an excess of producing-power, after exhibiting itself in a comparatively trifling glut of actual manufactured goods, shows its "waste" in the form of "unemployed" labour and capital, which operate in some measure as a check upon further application of labour and capital. In the latter, no such natural check is provided. Small quantities of capital, unable to enter manufacture with any reasonable prospect of success, may embark in distribution, especially in retail trade, with some hope of attracting to their businesses a fair proportion of the trade of others. It is not easy for a new business to succeed even in retail trade, but it is less difficult than in manufacture. The same amount of business may thus come to be divided among a larger number of persons. It may even supply a livelihood to all, on the single condition that the margin of profit in each sale is larger; which means, in a period of falling wholesale prices, that retail prices fall more slowly and more slightly. It can scarcely be doubted that this is a true description of the actual phenomena exhibited in distributive trade. The assumption commonly made by statesmen, and even by economists, that the consumer gains the advantage of the full decline of wholesale prices, and that such decline is therefore a matter of comparative indifference, is unwarranted. The cautious opinion expressed by J. S. Mill has been closely borne out by the experience of the last twenty years. "Retail price, the price paid by the actual consumer, seems to feel very slowly and imperfectly the effects of competition: and where competition does exist, it often, instead of lowering prices, merely divides the higher prices among a larger number of dealers." *

* "Principles of Political Economy," vol. ii., ch. iv. § 3.

In other words, an increased proportion of the prices paid by consumers goes to support agents, middle-men, shopkeepers, and their dependents, who thus receive a growing share of the national income paid for services of distribution. Without seeking to disparage the value of genuine services of necessary distribution, I may point out that this diseased swelling of labour and capital in distributive trade represents from the social standpoint a waste of power strictly analogous to the "unemployment" in manufacture, though different in the concrete aspect it assumes. In distribution, the waste does not for the most part show itself as "unemployed" and "unpaid" capital and labour, but as unnecessary reduplication of distributive machinery. In any scientific treatment of the "unemployed" question, this form of waste must rank as an important aspect of the social malady.

§ 13. False Assumption that all Power to Consume Must be Exercised.

The business man readily admits the existence of an excess of general producing-power in forms of capital and labour which are either unemployed or wastefully employed. But many economic theorists, misled by loose deductive reasoning, still persist in their denial of a phenomenon which stares the practical man in the face. It is not possible, they urge, that a general excess of capital and labour could exist, for these are the sole requisites of production, and since everything that is produced can find a market at a price, whatever can be produced will be produced, and whatever is produced will be consumed. Now, this line of reasoning is thoroughly fallacious. Since all business is the exchange of commodities for commodities, it is evident that some one possesses the power to consume whatever can be produced. It may also be asserted that, since the desires of man are unlimited, and many keenly felt wants remain unsatisfied, there exists a desire to consume whatever can be produced. But in order to an "effective demand" the power to consume and the desire to consume must be vested in the same persons. The denial by economists of the possibility of general excess of producing-power involves the assumption of this coincidence. This assumption is, however, false. Those who draw profit, interest, and rents from modern manufactures are thereby vested with *the power* to consume huge quantities of cotton and other textile wares, of coals, hardware, pottery, etc., but they have *the desire* to consume a comparatively small quantity of these commodities. "But," it may be urged, "they will have the desire to consume other commodities, and in order to obtain these they will exchange their superfluous cotton and iron goods with others who want to consume these articles." This, however, is not the case. After a certain tolerably high accustomed standard of consumption has been attained in cotton and iron wares, and in other articles for which these are exchanged, there still remains a large surplus power to consume which has no desire behind it to convert it into effectual demand.

§ 14. Is Desire to Consume the only Motive to Production?

It has generally seemed to economists of the last two generations a sufficient refutation of the theory of overproduction to assert that it is impossible, and to assume that this impossibility is proved by asking what motive prompts a person to produce except the desire to consume what is produced or its equivalent. "Each may not want more of what he himself produces, but each wants more of what some other produces, and by producing what the other wants, hopes to obtain what the other produces. There will always be consumption for everything which can be produced, until the wants of all who possess the means of producing are completely satisfied and the production will not increase any further." * Now though it must be allowed that a desire to consume is in general the motive force behind production, it does not operate so closely and so generally as to preclude the waste of over-production. A great many persons in whose hands rests the control of industry are not regulated in the quantity of production which they set on foot by the quantity of consumption which they desire, nor indeed does the desire to consume form the whole or the chief part of their conscious motive in their work of production.

§ 15. Does all "Saving" Give Increased Employment?

Mill assumes that all who own the power to consume want to consume all they can and to do so without delay.

Now, a large part of the power to consume is in the hands of those who have not the desire to consume. What, then, do these men desire to do? They desire to save. But saving, if we look behind the operation of putting money in a bank, means paying labour to set up plant, machinery, and other material forms of capital. But does not this give as much employment to capital and labour as the same power used to demand consumables? Quite

* J. S. Mill, "Unsettled Questions," p. 49.

true, the "saving" which employs labour to build a factory
and stock it with machinery will cause as much employment as the same amount of spending, though not more
employment, as J. S. Mill sought to maintain.   Moreover,
in the one case, when the money is "spent" there is
nothing to show for it, in the other case there is a factory
and machinery. But when our theoretic friend goes on
to assume that this factory can be profitably worked, and
that the work it affords signifies a net increase of employment both of labour and capital, he jumps to a conclusion which is quite unwarranted.   It can only be
profitably worked on one of two suppositions.   It may by
successful competition obtain the orders which would have
gone to another factory, ousting from employment the
capital and labour there engaged.   In this case it is clear
that no general increase of employment has taken place.
An individual has made good his "saving," but has done
so by negativing the previous "saving" of some one else;
the productive power of the community is increased, but
no more actual production than before is brought about.

The other supposition is that the demand for the class
of commodities which the factory makes will be greater
in the future, and that more capital and labour can
therefore be employed in the trade.   So far as this
supposition is valid, the "saving" is socially useful, and,
indeed, necessary; but it should be plainly recognised that
the dependence of capital and labour for employment
upon a rising standard of consumption places an absolute
limit at any given time upon socially useful saving.

It is therefore not true that the existence of a general
desire for increased consumption is any sufficient guarantee
that too much saving will not take place.   Even if it be

allowed that the ultimate object of persons who save is always the desire to consume an increased quantity in the future, this individual policy may and does result in a congestion of forms of capital which is suicidal from the collective point of view. In a society composed of A, B, C, D, E, F, any three, say A B C, might save as much as they liked, or each and all might save a definite proportion of their income, but any policy of the individual members which collectively exceeded this aggregate would be wasteful. Yet it might be quite possible that all individuals in this over-saving community were actuated by a genuine desire to consume largely in some distant future.

An individual may save any proportion of his income, provided he can induce others to spend their income and give him liens upon their present property or future production. But the proportion of a community's income which it can save and usefully store up in plant, machinery and other forms of capital is strictly limited by the rate of current or prospective consumption. Only a very small proportion of "saving" can profitably be invested in forms of capital that fructify in the distant future; the current or immediately prospective rate of consumption determines pretty closely the proportion of current income which can be usefully saved.

§ 16. *Excessive Forms of Capital do Exist.*

To the suggestion that an excess of saving is possible it is often deemed a sufficient answer to point to the infinitude of human wants and the new industrial enterprises which they can vitalise. Why, it is urged, should you assume that any trade will be over-stocked with new-saved capital, when the self-interest of savers will naturally lead them to prefer new uses. With the pure theory of this answer I have no quarrel. If all the "saved" incomes do in fact take shape in fixed forms of capital which supply increased consumption-goods in the shape of new public or private comforts and conveniences to the present or even to the next generation, we can thoroughly approve this saving : it is no cause of diminished employment.

Well, it may be said, does that not settle the matter? Are there not ample opportunities for the supply of new or improved public and private needs? Are our towns as well-built, commodious and beautiful as they might be? Are they perfectly supplied with water, lighting, transport, and other services? Could not public education provide a good field of investment for capital and labour both on the material and intellectual planes? Is it not self-evident that without passing the barrier of wholesome personal conveniences a vast and ever-growing number of good and reasonable wants remain unsatisfied because there is no capital and labour directed to their satisfaction? How in the face of this can over-saving be possible? Still more how can it be asserted to actually exist?

The answer is that a sufficient portion of new savings does not in fact seek these new avenues of socially useful investment, that a large proportion of it does flow into channels which are admittedly full, and that when this congestion is made manifest, much fresh "saving" instead of seeking new fields of investment accumulates in the hands of bankers and other persons. That portion of new savings which embodies itself in forms of capital that satisfy new wants is both morally and economically justified : that portion which embodies itself in the socially useless multiplication of existing forms of capital is harmless as regards employment so long as it continues to embody itself thus, but when by clogging the wheels of industry it stops the machinery and checks the investment of new "savings", it contributes to that state of under-employment and under-production which we call "tradedepression."

§ 17. The Theoretic Limit of Socially Useful Forms of Capital.

The theory that all new savings should and must find socially useful employment is contradicted by the facts. It is also unsound as a theory. Those who urge it show no motive force sufficient to compel new savings to invest themselves in socially useful ways. The individual saver does not want to raise the general level of consumption, he simply wants to find a remunerative investment for his capital. This he can often find, and still oftener thinks he can find, in setting up new forms of capital in trades which are already sufficiently provided for the supply of current consumption. No guarantee can be offered to him that that heterogeneous body of consumers called the public will pay him a higher rate of interest for putting his savings into untried ventures which shall stimulate and satisfy a new want.

Public improvements of an enduring order do indeed absorb a large and a growing quantity of new saving. But even here the quantity of capital which the most enlightened public body could safely apply, with reasonable regard to social, industrial, and other changes in the future, is strictly limited at any given time. A lavish expenditure with a view to a far distant consumption would often be a wasteful and an antisocial policy.

Indeed, as matters actually stand, such capital expenditure by public bodies is very limited, and there are no sufficient economic powers to drive the requisite proportion of new savings into the ideally correct channels. Hence the frequent congestion of all ordinary channels of investment, and the excess of loanable capital. It is quite possible that as large a proportion of our present general income as is now "saved" might under different economic conditions be advantageously applied in forms of new capital. But as matters actually stand some of it represents "oversaving" and brings about the state of congestion and stoppage of industry which has for one of its leading aspects the malady of "unemployment."

§ *18. How Excessive Forms of Capital Stop Production.*

Our saving class is therefore not necessarily causing an increase of "employment" by paying workers to put up more factories instead of using their moneys to demand consumables. So long as the "saving" is actually in progress—*i.e.*, so long as the factory and machinery are being made—the net employment of the community is just as large as if the money were spent to demand commodities; more labour is engaged in making factories, less in working them. But after the new factories are made, they can only be worked on condition that there is an increase of consumption correspondent to the increase of producing-power—*i.e.*, on condition that a sufficient number of persons are actuated by motives different from those which animated the "saving" class, and will consent to give validity to the saving of the former by "spending" on commodities an increased proportion of their incomes.) Where no such expectation is realised, an attempt to "operate" the new factories does not give any net increase of employment, it only gluts the markets, drives down prices, closes the weaker factories, imparts irregularity to work, and generally disorganises trade. The frequent recurrence of these phenomena in most departments of trade is the strongest presumptive evidence of an attempt of the capitalist classes to place and to operate more capital than is required to maintain the current flow of consumption. An individual may be a rich miser, a community cannot. To the average reasonable man it is a self-evident fact that a community cannot advantageously save more than a certain proportion of its annual income, unless for the express purpose of consuming a larger proportion at some not distant date.

§ 19.   The Fallacy that Saving Implies no Reduced Consumption.

The economist is, however, too often blinded by the acceptance of a strange sophism to the affect that "saving implies no reduction in current consumption,") a wild notion which is due to a failure to analyse the process of saving. The following simple refutation of this theory will suffice. Suppose the case of two economic' communities, each with a net annual income of £1,500,000,000. One nation spends the whole, saving nothing; this means that, after providing against wear and tear of existing plant, all the productive energy is devoted to producing "consumables" which are consumed. The other nation "saves" £200,000,000 annually: this means that, after the same provision for wear and tear, two-fifteenths of the productive energy is devoted, not to producing "consumables," but to setting up new plant, machinery, and unfinished goods, which are, in their form or their economic position, not consumable, and which are, in fact, not consumed. It would seem unnecessary to thus demonstrate that the consumption of the latter nation amounted to £1,300,000,000 (*i.e.*, that 15—2 = 13), were it not for the general prevalence of the notion that saving implies no reduction in consumption. Adam Smith is perhaps chiefly responsible for the misconception, by urging that "What is annually saved is as regularly consumed as what is annually spent, and nearly in the same time too, but it is consumed by a different set of people." * The heart of the fallacy, which has been effectively exposed by various writers, consists in failing to perceive that the difference between "spending" and "saving" is that the former, as an economic cause, causes "consumables" to be made, while the latter, so far as it finds an embodiment in actual forms of capital, causes "non-consumables" to be made. The forms of capital which represent "saving" correspond to the extra consumption which would have taken place if the persons saving had not saved, but had applied the money in demand for consumables.

§ 20. *The Limit to Social Saving.—No Limit to Individual Saving.*

This simple truth that real saving implies diminished consumption for the time being is the kernel of a true understanding of the" unemployed" question. If we find labour and

* "Wealth of Nations," p. 1496, McCulloch; *cf.* Mill's "Political Economy," vol. i. ch. v. § 6.

capital unemployed in our manufactures, if we find them wastefully employed in our distributing industry, it can only mean an undue diminution of consumption, or, in other words, an attempt to establish as " savings " a larger number of forms of capital than are economically required to assist in maintaining current or prospective consumption.

These results of over-saving are not, of course, made manifest at once. So long as the over-saving is being stored in new plant or machinery and so long as this new plant is engaged in turning out increased supply of goods, there is no reduction of employment and no fall of general prices. It is when the admitted glut of goods checks further investment and over-saving can find no vent that prices fall, production is slackened and unemployment shows itself.

The failure to give proper recognition to the obvious fact that the quantity of serviceable forms of capital at the several stages of production is absolutely limited by the rates at which consumable goods are drawn out of the industrial machine, arises from the refusal to consider industry from the social organic standpoint. Because an individual or a class of individuals can " save" without any other limit than that imposed by the necessity of living, it has been wrongly supposed that the same rule holds good of a whole community. This blind individualistic conception of industry was aided by the recognition of the moral and material value which attaches to the exercise of effectual thrift by individual members of a society, and which within the limits imposed by the aggregate consumption must be recognised as necessary and beneficial to society. Although the famous dictum of Adam Smith that " the study of his own advantage naturally, or rather necessarily, leads him to prefer that employment which is most advantageous to the society," * has been largely replaced in modern minds by a perception that "the mere conflicts of private interests will never produce a well-ordered commonwealth of labour,"† the implications of this new doctrine have not been properly digested. Many of those who most fully recognise the necessity of imposing restraints upon "conflicts of private interests" in the competition of the labour-market and in the sale of goods, still hold that the selfishness of individual "savers" can be relied upon to secure the most economical disposition of capital at the several points of the industrial machine. We have seen that this is not true in fact, that the operation of saving individuals under the existing industrial dispensation leads to a wasteful accumulation of forms of capital. It remains to ask, Why should this be so; why should the free selfish action of saving individuals disturb the right adjustment between "saving" and "spending" from the standpoint of the community? Why should it be possible for us to endeavour to establish new capital to the extent of £200,000,000 a year, when £150,000,000 might, perhaps, suffice to supply the current rate of consumption, increased by £50,000,000?

§ 21. How Self-interest of Individuals Causes Social Waste of Capital.

We have already seen that in retail trade the self-interest of individual traders may and does lead them to establish a far larger number of shops than are required for the effective distribution of commodities in a district.

* "Wealth of Nations," book iv., chap. ii.
† Article on Political Economy in "Encyclopædia Britannica."

Similarly in manufacture it is often to the interest of a capitalist to set up and to work new spinning-mills or iron-works, although there may already exist enough mills and works to supply every possible demand, provided he sees a fair prospect of getting away from his competitors a sufficient proportion of the trade. Nor is it an adequate reply to say that the new-comer can only get the trade by producing a better or a cheaper article, and that in this way the community, as a body of consumers, is advantaged by his action. In the first place, this statement is not true; it is commonly by superiority in the arts of competition, which do not necessarily involve superiority of production, that the modern business firm is able to get business. Secondly, even supposing that the new capital is made effective by some trifling economy in methods of production, it by no means follows that the consuming public gains by the lowering of prices, or gains to a corresponding extent. For we have already seen that the constant cutting of prices in manufacturing trades has been a chief operative cause of the multiplication of middle-men and retailers, whose maintenance prevents a fall of retail prices equivalent to the fall of wholesale prices. Lastly, the fall of retail prices to the consuming public must not be taken as the just and final test and measure of a net industrial gain to the community. The gain may be bought too dearly if it involves, as it often does, a large and unforeseen displacement of capital and labour in earlier use, the vested interests of which receive neither compensation nor consideration under the stern rule of competitive trade. This is no plea for conservatism in industry, or for the rejection of new and improved forms of machinery and method. It is only designed as a protest against the waste of the wrecking policy in modern commerce, by which old businesses are ruined by the speculative operation of new competitors who bring with them no intrinsic superiority of production sufficient to compensate the destruction of capital value and the disturbance of employment which they cause.

§ 22. *The Difference between Individual and Social Economy.*

It is important to recognise that an economy of production which is sufficient to enable a new firm to cut prices and to get business is not necessarily an economy at all from the standpoint of the whole commercial community. If a new firm can set up plant to produce one-tenth per cent. more cheaply the goods which are now supplied by other firms, it will clearly be to its interest to do so. But if an established firm discovered this new cheaper method of production, it would only set up the new plant on condition that the cheapening of production was sufficiently great to compensate for the cancelling of the old plant with which it had operated hitherto. The new firm would not take into consideration the cancelling of old capital, the established firm would set this against the advantages of the new method, and would only adopt the new method, if there was a *net* economy. Now the industrial community, which includes all its members and their property, may, for the purpose of this argument, be regarded as the owners of all the forms of capital; their net interest then is measured not by the advantage of the new competing firm, but by that of the firm which owns the older forms of capital which it is proposed to displace. It follows then that in a competitive society, it may be the distinct interest of individuals to set up "savings" in new forms of capital, which, having no regard to the destruction of the value of older forms of capital, confer no net economic advantage on the community.

This free play of individual self-interest in saving leads to a purchase of each step of industrial progress by a most expensive cancelment of old "savings." Since obsolete forms do not at once perish, but struggle to keep the breath of industrial life and to play their accustomed part, we find in existence at any given time a large excess of plant of various kinds beyond what is fully utilised for actual work of production.

§ 23. *A Nation is not a Community.*

In ascribing necessary limits to the "savings" of a community, it must be borne in mind that in mode.n industry a "nation" is by no means coterminous with a "community." Every year more and more the whole body of nations, which are related by close ties in common world-markets, or are otherwise in direct or indirect commercial relations with one another, must be regarded as a single commercial community. This being so, it is clear that no absolute limit is set at any given time to the "savings" of a single nation, other than the total field of investment of the industrial world. It would therefore follow that not only is there no theoretic limit to the proportion of his income which any individual Englishman might legitimately save, but that no limit could be placed upon the proportion of the national income which can be saved, provided that the surplus savings beyond what can find useful occupation in home trade dispose themselves in foreign countries. Since our enquiry into the facts of Unemployment was chiefly confined to England, it may seem that the wider causal treatment is not strictly relevant. It is indeed quite true that here as elsewhere, .in all industrial problems, the international factor is of so great importance that a full scientific investigation should stand upon a basis of international statistics. These we cannot yet, obtain with any degree of accuracy. There is, however, we have seen, a general agreement both among business men and scientific experts that those phenomena of depressed trade which we study chiefly in England and America are simultaneously visible in different shapes and degrees throughout those other countries which make up the industrial world. Since the money-market is the most perfect of world-markets, the unimpeachable testimony to a large and general glut of loanable capital affords conclusive evidence that the "unemployed" question on the side of capital is of general application. On the side of labour the gigantic armaments maintained by certain continental countries absorb large masses of labour which would otherwise swell the ranks of "unemployed" or displace those at present in work. Many structural differences of industrial society in less developed countries conceal the waste, which there is every reason to believe exists.

Lastly it does not devolve on me to prove that all the phenomena which we have found in England exist elsewhere, in order to show that there exists "over-saving" and an excess of forms of capital in the whole international community. If there were no "unemployment" of capital and labour in England, that would not prove there were

no unemployment in the whole community, but might be
attributable to the superior ability of English capital and
labour to find employment. But if in any considerable
part of the industrial community of nations such general
"unemployment" or excess of producing-power does exist,
it is proof of the over-saving of the community, whether
it is also found in other nations of the community or not.

§ 24.   The Motives of Under-Consumption. A Natural Law of Consumption.

But thus far I have only explained the mechanism of
over-capitalisation, the central fact of the unemployed
question. What are the motive forces which act upon
individuals impelling them to a line of action which, from
the wider standpoint of the community, is uneconomical?
Why does the free play of individual interests fail to
secure the interest of the whole community?

The answer to this vital question is found in the region
of Distribution. The reason why attempts are made by
individuals to establish more forms of capital than are
socially required, is that they possess certain elements of
income which are not earned by effort, and which are therefore
not required to satisfy any present legitimate wants. In spite
of all attempts to make an artificial severance between a
"producing" and a "consuming" class, the natural relation
between production and consumption, between effort and
satisfaction, exercises a strong influence in the social economy.
It is possible for individuals and for classes who draw large
incomes *alieni vultus sudore*, or without any considerable contribution of effort, to be large and profuse consumers. But, after
all, the law which relates effort to satisfaction is a "natural"
law, which, finding its simplest expression in the physical

fact that a man cannot eat and digest a good dinner unless he has made some output of physical energy in exercise, penetrates in some unseen way the whole region of consumption, denying satisfaction that is not compensated by some corresponding personal effort. This "natural" law finds an economical expression in the fact that an attempt to be a very large consumer and a very small producer in the long run defeats itself, and, when it cannot by force of social circumstances stimulate production, it limits consumption.

This, interpreted into simple language, means that a man who draws a large income without working for it cannot and does not spend it. This will seem to some a strange assertion, at variance with the lavish luxury imputed to and practised by many members of the upper unemployed class, but it is literally true. Though the bulk of the painful abstinence and thrift in our modern communities is practised by the working and poorer trading and professional classes, the bulk of the "saving" is effected by the wealthy. The accumulated savings of the manual workers of the country, even if we place to their account the whole of the £200,000,000, which in round figures represents the total capital of savings banks, trade unions, benefit, building, co-operative and mutual societies of every kind, does not amount to more than two per cent. of the total accumulated wealth of the country. Although we have no means of exactly apportioning the ownership of capital value among the various classes of the community, we know that a large proportion represents the accumulation of the surplus income of the wealthy classes after their wholesome and even their luxurious wants are satisfied. The portentous growth of the capital wielded by a few successful business men in America affords an extreme case of the self-accumulative power of capital. There are on both sides of the Atlantic a small number of families whose most profuse expenditure yet leaves an enormous surplus income to accumulate. "I can do nothing with my income," said Mr. J. J. Astor, "but buy more land, build more houses, and lend money on mortgage. In short, I am found with the necessaries of life, and more than that I cannot get out of my money." The absorption of interest and the specialisation of activities required for the successful practice of money-making are commonly such as to leave undeveloped or to disable the capacities for spending even upon the lower planes of material enjoyment. Hence "we see as a rule that men who have made money in business are not great spenders of it in the present, and have often no other notion of spending it than to make new businesses to bring them in future returns." *

Turning from these leviathans to the merely wealthy classes, we find most of them living well within their incomes and furnishing large sums for investment. It would, I think, be pretty safe to conclude that a very large percentage of incomes received as rents and interest are not used for current expenditure, but are left to grow by compound interest. Since these elements of income are not earned by present efforts, they are not, as a rule, required to satisfy present desires.

In thus stating my position, I do not wish to be understood as denying the utility or even the "productive power" of that abstinence which may rightly rank as "present effort" in the case of the savings of less wealthy

* Dr. Bonar, "Philosophy and Political Economy," p. 222.

members of the community. My point is simply this, that a large proportion of "new capital" does not represent "saving" due to painful abstinence, careful postponement of present to future use, but represents the merely automatic accumulation of an idle surplus of income after all genuine and wholesome needs are fully satisfied. Where incomes flow in, yielding a power of consumption wholly disproportionate to the output of personal effort, a natural tendency to "save" is manifested, which is sharply distinguishable from the reasonable "saving" made out of legitimate earnings. It is this automatic "saving" which upsets the balance between consumption and producing-power, and which from the social standpoint may be classed as "over-saving." No class of men whose "savings" are made out of their hard-won earnings is likely to oversave, for each unit of "capital" will represent a real want, a piece of legitimate consumption deferred. But where "savings" represent the top portion of large incomes, drawn from economic rents of land, profits of speculation, high interest of capital derived from monopolies, no natural limit is set upon the amount which is saved.

§ 25. Excess of Capital a Result of "Unearned" Incomes.

If this reasoning is correct, the over-capitalisation which is found to exist is identified with those elements of individual incomes which are unearned in the sense that their "incoming" is not attended by any corresponding "outgoing" of effort on the part of the recipient. This is no doubt largely an à priori argument, but it contains the only hypothesis which serves to explain the facts. This hypothesis may be formally summarised in the following terms. Modern machinery and methods of production have brought about a vast and continuous increase in the power of producing wealth: the rate of consumption has likewise risen, but less rapidly. This decrepancy in the pace of progress is manifested in the existence of a permanent surplus of producing-power—*i.e.*, though every producing-power implies the existence of a corresponding consuming-power the latter is not fully utilised. This failure to fully utilise consuming-power is due to the fact that much of it is owned by those who, having already satisfied all their strong present desires, have no adequate motive for utilising it in the present, and therefore allow it to accumulate.

§ 26. *No Repudiation of Uses of Individual Thrift.*

To all who have followed carefully the line of reasoning adopted here it ought to be manifest that no depreciation of the merit and uses of individual "thrift" is intended or conveyed. But so firmly implanted in the mind of most men is the individualist conception of the commercial community, that they are exceedingly apt to transfer the limit set upon the "saving" of a community to the case of an individual. The temptation to defend an orthodox position in "economics" by representing its assailants as engaged in an insidious attack upon the character and moral habits of the members of the working classes has proved too powerful for many critics. It may therefore be well to conclude this chapter by a distinct pronouncement to the effect that an acceptance of the doctrine, that the quantity of socially useful "saving" for a community at a given time is limited, does not in any

EFFECT OF UNDER-CONSUMPTION

shape or degree impair the obligation of individuals to make provision out of their current incomes for future contingencies of sickness, unemployment, old age, etc., nor does it lend the least suggestion of disparagement to any policy of "saving," either on the part of an individual or a community, which takes the shape of deferred consumption. Such right distribution of spending-power over periods of time belongs to the conduct of every rational man or society of men. The only limit is that imposed upon the total fund of sound investment at any given time by the quantity of current consumption in the community, and the impossibility of forecasting and providing for any save a very small proportion of the consumption of the future.

APPENDIX B.

Effect of Under-Consumption on Employment.

It seems best to reserve one important point in the Economics of Saving for separate statement here. The admission made in the text of this chapter that over-saving or the establishment of socially unnecessary forms of capital gives as much employment while it is going on as spending does, and that the attempt to work an excessive number of factories, etc., may for a time yield full employment, is liable to be misunderstood. It may appear that, after all, no net increase of employment would be caused by a well-adjusted balance between saving and spending, and that the malady is only one affecting the distribution of employment, and not the total volume; that the only effect of over-saving is to balance periods of under-employment and over-employment against one another.

Now I think this conclusion is not well founded. The following line of illustration will, I think, make it apparent that a net loss of employment over a long period is caused by under consumption and not merely a maldistribution of employment.

In order to test the case, take a community with stable population where there has existed a right economic relation between forms of capital and rate of consumption. Suppose an attempt is initiated to increase saving by abstention from consumption of some class of goods, say, Cotton. Increased saving has no legitimate economic channel, if we suppose this parsimonious policy is to continue and not to be balanced by an early period of abnormal spending. Since no trade requires increase of capital, the new savings may as well be invested in the form of new cotton mills as in any other way. Let us suppose that the over-saving of the first year is capitalised in this form. What has occurred during this first year is that an increased employment of capital and labour in making cotton mills has balanced a diminished employment in making cotton goods. Assuming an absolute fluidity of capital and labour, the net employment for the community is not affected by the change. People have simply been paid to make cotton mills instead of to make cotton goods. At the end of the year there exists an excess of cotton mills over what would have been required if consumption of cotton goods had stood firm, a double excess over what is needed to supply the now reduced demand for cotton goods. If it seems unfair to anyone that I should apply the over-saving to the only trade where the demand is absolutely reduced, I can only reply that it simplifies the argument and makes no real difference in its validity. If we assumed the "saving" to be equally distributed among all trades, then at the end of the year all trades would be to a minor degree in the same condition as the cotton trade is according to my illustration.

If savers were mad enough to continue this policy, preferring the growing ownership of useless cotton-mills to the satisfaction of consuming commodities, the process might continue indefinitely, without reducing or affecting in any way the aggregate employment of labour and capital. It would simply mean that a number of persons take their satisfaction in seeing new cotton-mills rising and going to decay.

But it is conceivable that in the second year of over-saving, the savers instead of continuing to pay people to put up more mills might employ people to operate the excess of cotton-mills, lending their money to buy raw material and to pay wages. Cotton goods which *ex hypothesi* can find no markets are thus accumulated. If the savers chose to take their pleasure in such a way, they might go on indefinitely without the aggregate of employment of capital or labour being affected. If they continued this impolicy for a twelvemonth, we should say that whereas in the first year they saved useless mills, in the second year they saved useless cotton goods. In neither the first nor the second year is there any net increase or decrease of employment due to the new policy of saving. In fact, assuming sanity of individual conduct, affairs would work out differently. Admitting an attempt to work the surplus mills, the actual overproduction of goods could not proceed far. Let us assume savers to use, throughout, the agency of Banks, which are to find investment for their savings. Suppose the Banks, not realising the mode of this new saving, have invested the first year's savings in superfluous cotton mills. These cotton mills or others in the next year cannot continue to work without advances from Banks, since they are unable to effect profitable sales. Soon after the beginning of the second year the Banks will refuse to make further advances for over-production: markets being congested and prices falling, the demand for bank accommodation will grow, but banks will not be justified in making advances. Now the weaker mills must stop work, general short time follows, and the result is an employment of labour and forms of capital. This is the first effect of the attempt to over-save upon employment. We have now for the first time a reduction of the aggregate of production. The result of reduced employment (under-production) will be a reduction of real incomes. This will tend to proceed until the reduced reward of saving (real interest) gradually restores the right proportion of saving to spending —a very slow and wasteful cure.

It thus appears that so long as " saving " can be vested in new forms of capital, whether these are socially useful or not, no net reduction of employment is caused, the portion of income which is "saved" employs as much labour as, though not more than, that which is "spent," but when the machinery of production is so glutted that attempted saving takes shape in the massing of "loanable capital" unable to find an investment, the net production and the net employment of labour in the community is smaller than it would have been had saving been confined to the minimum required by the needs of society.

From the standpoint of "employment" the injury done by over-saving is thus seen to consist not in the over-production of plant or goods but in the condition of under-production which follows the financial recognition of this glut. The real waste of power of capital and labour is measured by the period and the intensity of the under-production in which forms of capital and labour stand idle.

Briefly, the order of causation is this :

Under-consumption or over-saving causes over-capitalisation, first in forms of fixed capital, then in a glut of goods ; the glut checks the investment of loanable capital ; this check restricts production and a period of under-production with low prices ensues.

Thus it appears that the immediate cause of the under-production and unemployment is the inability of would-be savers and investors to find any forms of capital capable of embodying their savings. It makes no immediate difference as regards aggregate employment in the community, whether incomes are spent in demand for consumption-goods or for plant or for production-goods : so long as savers who hold money-tokens are able to apply them anywhere in the actual field of industry they equally stimulate production and employment, but when misdirection compels them to withhold their application, production falls off and unemployment ensues.

It is the identification of this refusal to apply the money-tokens of saving with lack of confidence that induces economists like Bagehot to explain bad trade by lack of confidence. This lack of confidence is shown * to be merely the subjective side of lack of openings for investment, an objective fact due to over-saving.

* See Chapter VII.

CHAPTER VI

THE ECONOMIC REMEDY

§ 1. The Remedy lies in a Reformed Distribution of Consuming Power.

THIS is the only rationale of the simultaneous unemployment of labour, land, and capital which forms the problem of the "unemployed." Under-consumption is the economic cause of unemployment. The only remedy, therefore, which goes to the root of the evil is a raising of the standard of consumption to the point which shall fully utilise the producing-power, after making due allowance for such present "saving" as is economically needed to provide for further increase of consumption in the future. If the analysis of causes in the last chapter is correct, this remedy can only be made operative by a line of policy which shall affect the ownership of increased consuming-power.

Unfortunately this last conclusion was not admitted by economic writers whose diagnosis of trade-disease was in close accord with that taken here. The brilliant analysis of Malthus in particular was never rebutted, but it could be disregarded safely by the economists of his day, because he used it in defence of the luxury of the classes. Malthus saw that the over-saving of the wealthy was the direct economic force which kept trade back. His remedy was an increase of luxurious expenditure. But this, even were it otherwise desirable, is wholly impracticable. We have seen that the motives which induce the wealthy to withhold the present use of consuming-power are natural and necessary. A piece of academic advice, unbacked by any economic force, is absolutely futile. The owners of "unearned" elements of income, as we see, *must* accumulate capital which from the social standpoint is excess. A more natural distribution of consuming-power, under which the power to consume shall be accompanied by the desire to consume—not, as now, severed from it— is the only possible remedial policy.

§ 2. *Lines of Social Policy. Taxation of "Unearned" Income.*

Towards this policy, parties of social progress are slowly gravitating. Unfortunately their path is lighted by no clear intellectual conceptions, and they move with hesitant, uneven, staggering steps, often by circuitous routes, along a road which should be recognised as clear, straight, and fairly smooth. The policy of progressive consumption has two direct lines of advance which may here be briefly indicated.

The surplus of consuming-power in the hands of the rich may be "unearned" by its owners, but it is not, for all that, "unearned." Part of it—for example, the growing value of town lands—is earned by public effort, and forms a property designed for public consumption in the support of wholesome public life.

§ 3.   *Various forms of "Social Property" Amenable to Taxation.*

"It certainly is true that any increase in the rental value or selling value of land is due, not to the exertions and sacrifices of the owners of the land, but to the exertions and sacrifices of the community. It is certainly true that economic rent tends to increase with the growth of wealth and population, and that thus a larger and larger share of the product of industry tends to pass into the hands of the owners of land, not because they have done more for society, but because society has greater need of that which they control." *   Here then is indicated a large property "earned" by the work of the community which might be usefully consumed by the community. .But these land values by no means exhaust and probably do not form the largest . portion of that annual property directly created by public effort or the pressure of public needs. Part of the profits of all monopolies or protected businesses and of many businesses not formally protected but assisted by some dependence upon land, some advantage of position or vicinity to markets, is clearly due to the same social causes as are operative in the direct growth of land values. Profits obtained from various branches of local services, many departments of the transport trades and of retail distribution are often enhanced by this extraneous support. In some cases the profits which thus arise go to swell rent, as is largely the case with the profits of shops in advantageous positions, in other cases sufficient competition, direct or indirect, may survive to enable the consuming

* Professor Francis Walker ("First Lessons in Political Economy").

public to reap the advantage in lower prices. But any one who goes over the most remunerative kinds of industry will find that many of these derive their character from dependence upon natural or legal monopoly. The strong position of such a trade as brewing is explained by a combination of natural and legal monopoly. In all such trades elements of profits are apt to emerge which are not the necessary interest upon capital, nor results of skill in production or enterprise in management, but are simply due to a power of monopoly or in other words to the pressure of public needs. Even where no direct assistance is derived from natural or legal monopoly, a combination of capital strong enough to crush out or keep down effective competition may obtain so strong a control of the market through a " ring," a " syndicate," " trust," or other business structure, as to exercise a similar power of taxing the public for its private profit. All this body of rents and profits represents a property made by public efforts and needs which might, wherever it can be discovered, legitimately pass into the public possession.

In many cases it may be difficult, in some perhaps impossible, to discriminate economic rents and monopoly profits from those growths of value which are needed for the maintenance of the private effort and enterprise which co-operated to produce them. But economic analysis discloses the fact that there does exist a large fund of "unearned" incomes, the private ownership of which is justified neither by natural "right" nor by expediency, which could economically be taken by the public and used for public purposes. These unearned elements of income are not needed to induce the application of individual effort in those who at present own them; they are needed for the improvement and enlargement of public life.

Our civic and, in general, our public life, is narrow, meagre, inefficient, and undignified in comparison with what it ought to be, if the wealth due to public effort was wisely and economically laid out in the public service. Taxation, or State assumption on equitable terms, of properties whose increasing values are due to public activity and public need, to be administered in the supply of common wants and the enrichment of the common life, is likely to be of material assistance in raising the general standard of consumption. The adoption of progressive taxation of accumulated wealth through the Death Duties is based on an instinctive recognition that this assertion of a public claim is both just and expedient. The same is true of the progressive income-tax, so adjusted as to secure for purposes of public use that portion of the income of the well-to-do which otherwise would materially assist to swell the excess of accumulated forms of capital.

The direct and progressive taxation of ground rents and values, so far as they can be ascertained, would accord with this policy. The economist, while insisting upon the necessity of securing to all private investors whose "saving" is needed to furnish capital, the market price of such saving, i.e., the minimum interest required to draw sufficient capital into the several channels of production, would sanction the taxation of dividends which exceeded that necessary limit. The application of this purely economic principle would of course be liable to be overruled by considerations of practical politics. At present many elements of "unearned" income accrue in the course of private business which cannot be assessed, and even in the case of public companies, the possibility of evading heavy taxation by watering stock, distributing bonuses and by other means of concealing profits, would have to be considered by statesmen guided by an economic policy. Economists will declare that these elements of income are a legitimate object of taxation wherever they can be reached, in that they are the result of public activities and public needs. How far and in what ways they can best be reached are questions for politics as distinguished from economics.

These practical qualifications do not, however, impair the value of the light which economic analysis throws upon the paths of the progressive policy.

If the public mind once firmly fastens on the economic principle that taxation, in whatever way imposed, tends * to settle on the economic rent of land, high profits of monopolies and other "unearned" elements of individual income, it is likely that the assumption of public property by means of progressive taxation will be more rapid and more systematic than hitherto.

§ 4. Working-Class Movement for Higher Wages.

The other line of advance is the organised pressure of the working classes for an increasing proportion of the

---

* This tendency is of course in many instances thwarted or retarded by the effect of leases and other contracts and by various . forms of friction which impede the strictly "economic" settlement of taxation here indicated, imposing for a time new burdens upon those who are ill able to bear them. The tendency, however, of . practical politicians is to over-estimate the length of time taken by a tax to settle on rents.

national income, which they will use in raising their standard of consumption. By effective trade organisation they may raise wages, by co-operation of consumers they may expend their wages more economically, by organised use of the franchise they may secure such equality of educational and economic opportunities as will remove or abate the dangers of ignorance and destitution, which at present bar the progress of the rear-guard of labour. The low rate of interest and profits in many trades is no sufficient barrier to the wisely regulated pressure of trade-organisations for higher wages. Setting aside all consideration of the greater efficiency of higher paid labour, we cannot fail to see that the effective demand for higher wages tends like a tax to settle on unearned elements of income. A rise of wages, in a trade where profits lie at a minimum, tends to lower rents, or, in default of rent, by raising prices, falls upon those consumers whose money incomes will not be affected by a rise of prices.

§ 5. Increased Consumption gives Validity to Increased Saving.

Let it be clearly understood that this policy of increased consumption by the public and by the working classes of the country contains no repudiation either of the principle or the practice of saving. On the contrary, each rise of general consumption signifies, not merely an increased employment of labour, but of capital as well. A rise in the general standard of consumption is a demand for more saving and it alone can give economic validity to more saving, by enabling it to assist in the satisfaction of increased needs. The very gist of our analysis lay in the disclosure that every increase of effective saving was dependent upon an increase of consumption.

It is in a country where, new-felt needs are constantly clamouring for satisfaction, where men spend freely, as in the United States, that the growth of valid forms of capital is largest.

§ 6. *Effect of a Shorter Working-day upon Consumption. Cases where Output is Maintained.*

The pressure towards a shorter working-day must likewise be held to conduce, both in its direct and in its indirect influence, to the same end, the elevation of the general standard of consumption. It is true this may not hold of all trades and all circumstances. The plea for an Eight Hours Day on the ground that it will absorb the unemployed does not admit of general acceptance. In many occupations, as Mr. Rae and others have shown, the shorter working-day will simply mean an increased compression of labour, the same output being produced in an eight hours day as previously in a nine or ten hours day. In all cases where, either by this intensification of labour or by improved machinery and method, the shorter day is as productive as the longer day was formerly, there will be no absorption of "the unemployed" and no direct effect upon the aggregate volume of employment. This would probably be the result of shortening the hours of labour in some of the mining and metal industries, in those branches of textile and other manufactures where machinery is not yet perfected or speeded to full pitch, and in the bulk of the distributive trades. In these it is likely that a shorter day would be made as productive as a longer day.

§ 7.   *Where a Shorter Day Means a Smaller Output.*

But in many other departments of work there would be a loss of productivity by shortening the working day. In this case one of three things might happen. First: the former output might be maintained by reduction of the daily wage and an increase in the number of those employed at the lower wage. On this supposition there would be no increase in the total consumption of the working classes, no increase in the volume of employment, but only a distribution of the former volume of employment among a larger number of persons. It is quite conceivable that this might happen in the engineering and other trades, were trade unions able and willing to enforce their resolutions against the use of over-time. Since the absorption of the whole or a part of the unemployed would strengthen trade-organisation and improve the position of workers in bargaining with masters, it is considered unlikely that the shorter working-day, even in trades where the output was diminished, would be attended by an actual reduction in daily wages. Supposing the same wage was paid for the reduced product, one of two results would follow.

§ 8.   *Where the Cost of a Shorter Day comes out of Profits.*

In cases where profits were above the minimum required to maintain the continued application of capital, the former aggregate production would be maintained, the increased wages-bill being defrayed at the expense of profits. In this way monopoly profits, and other "un-earned" elements of income, which we have seen to be amenable to taxation, might pass to the workers in the shape of increased wages. Although the common belief of working men that the "eight-hours' day" or any other increased cost of production could be paid for out of profit does not admit the sweeping application it often receives, there are unquestionably many trades which in normal conditions could and actually would bear the "cost." In these cases the transfer of would-be profits and rents to wages in attainment of a shorter working-day for a larger number of workers would be directly instrumental in raising the consumption of the community, for if our former analysis be correct a far larger proportion of the wages than of the profits and rents will be spent upon consumables.

§ 9. Where the "Cost" Comes out of Higher Prices.

Again, there will be other cases where, trade competition being keen, profits are too low to bear the increased cost, but where prices might be raised and consumers made to bear the cost. This would be the case where international competition is excluded and where, as in the case of necessaries or prime comforts, the necessary rise of price would not appreciably affect consumption. The objection which is sometimes raised to the effect that such a rise of prices though it might benefit the workers in some trades would not benefit the whole body of workers since in their capacity of consumers they would suffer, does not seem convincing.

The rise of price will really operate in the same way as a new tax which it is sought to place upon wages, the real incidence of which may be tested by taking the position of the lowest-paid class of labour in the community. It can, I think, easily be seen that the "real wages" of this class cannot be reduced by a tax upon the money wage, even in the form of a rise of prices: if the prices of articles consumed by the "marginal" labourer are raised, his wages must rise to meet them. Similarly an attempt to tax other classes of labour with a strongly fixed standard of comfort will be resisted. In other words the higher prices will not ultimately injure the standard of comfort of the lower strata of workers but will tend to fall, like a tax, upon the unearned incomes which can afford to pay the higher prices. Skilled workmen with high wages or whose standards of comfort were not strongly fixed might suffer somewhat from the rise of prices, but most of the increased cost would ultimately settle upon "surplus" income.

§ *10.　Where International Competition Keeps down Profits and Prices.*

The third possibility lies in the trades where international competition presses keenly and where reduced hours would not be compensated by increased productivity of labour per hour. Here the normal result of pressing a shorter working-day on any other than an international basis would be to disable all weaker competitors from continuing in business, with the effect of reducing the total output of the trade and the total volume of employment. Some trades are certainly in such a case that reduced hours would imply an increased wages-bill which could neither be paid out of profits nor by raising prices: here the compulsory application of shorter hours (unless in pursuance of international policy) would reduce both the volume of consumption and of production, spoiling the trade.

All reasonable advocates of a general policy of shortening the working-day must make just allowance for trades in this last condition. With these important exceptions and modifications it is true that the shorter working-day will contribute to strengthen the economic position of the workers and to increase the proportion of consuming-power which falls into their hands. It will directly absorb a certain proportion of "unemployment." It will do away with certain irregularities of employment which are not truly inherent in the nature and conditions of the trade, but are due to the disturbing existence of a large margin of spare labour. By relieving to some degree the glut of the labour-market it will assist labour to organise more effectively and to raise the general standard of working-class consumption.

§ 11. Increased Leisure a Condition of Rising Consumption.

The indirect effects of a shorter working-day are not less important. Provided the increased leisure is not purchased by an injurious over-strain in the shorter working-day, the increased opportunities it will afford for the cultivation of unused faculties and the satisfaction of new tastes, will furnish an ever-growing stimulus towards an elevation of the standard of life. By yielding a continuous demand for the satisfaction of new, strong desires it will supply the moral force which, allied with improved intelligence and the more effective means of organisation which modern conditions of industry and of life afford, makes powerfully and persistently for enforcing the claims of the

working classes to a larger share of the aggregate consuming-power of the community.

§ 12.   A Summary of the "High Consumption" Policy.

Thus the recognition of "unemployment" as the labour
aspect of a wider economic problem—*viz.*, the excess of
productive power over the requirements of current consumption, supplies us for the first time with a sound practical
standard by which to test the worth of proposed remedies
and palliatives.

It furnishes a strong economic justification for the chief
lines of action which modern progressive parties have
instinctively taken. The transfer of economic rents and
monopoly profits from private owners to the public, whether
by taxation of incomes or by direct public assumption of
the functions of monopolist industries, is seen to contribute
to the enhancement of the aggregate consumption of the
community. Similar results attend the well-considered
endeavours of working classes, either by direct increase
of wages or by increased leisure, to increase the proportion
of the total wealth of the community, which falling to them
as wages shall be spent in raising the general standard
of working-class consumption.

§ 13.   This Policy involves no Social Danger.

But those who are not willing to admit the existence of
any large "unearned" elements of income, or who fear
lest this progressive taxation might encroach too far, are
needlessly alarmed. Assuming there existed no large
unearned elements of income, so long as there exists any
quantity of unutilised producing-power, labour, land, and

capital, which is under-employed, it does not seem reasonable to suppose that such taxation imposed upon owners of land and capital will reduce the aggregate income derived from such ownership. For since the direct result of this taxation is to increase the general consumption, such increase must in the nature of the case give increased employment to all the requisites of production. Hence it would appear that the quantity of land and capital for which rent, interest, and profit is paid will be larger than before, though the rate of the remuneration for the use of each piece of land or capital may be kept within moderate limits by taxation or by the pressure of labour-organisation. If there were no unearned elements of income they could not be taken by taxation and any attempt to tax socially necessary interest would defeat itself. The complexity of our industrial organism is such as to preclude me from here tracing out the exact *modus operandi* by which a new tax or an effective demand for higher wages must work. But if the principle be once firmly grasped that a demand for commodities is the only ultimate demand for the use of land, labour, and capital, then the existence of "unemployed" producing-power, is proof that increased consumption is possible without a reduction in the present income of any class of the community. The legitimacy of a "progressive" consumptive policy is not, therefore, dependent upon a theory of "economic monopolies," but has a separate justification.

CHAPTER VII

BIMETALLISM AND TRADE DEPRESSION

§ 1. The Industrial and Financial Sides of Business.

THE monetary or financial explanations of commercial crises and consequent depressions do not in the least invalidate this analysis, nor can they be accepted as substitutes for it. Every fact in the production, distribution, and exchange of commercial wealth has its book-keeping or financial side. For every change that takes place in the economic nature or the ownership of commercial goods there is some change in the ownership of money or of credit. There is some correspondence between the two classes of movements, but not an accurate one. Oscillations in the total quantity of money and of credit, changes in the distribution of its ownership may take place without any facts of corresponding size or character in industry. The operations of the money market furnish familiar examples. A company is floated, credit is manufactured by bankers and other persons, is imputed to certain persons and will for certain times and purposes perform the functions of money, without

any corresponding reality in the production of serviceable forms of value. This, however, though of extremely
great importance in the world of business, must be held
exceptional. In most cases, in all sound business, a
creation of forms of commercial value. has taken place
corresponding to the money or the credit, and there is
a parallelism in the distribution of ownership of the two.

The object of these remarks is to establish clearly the
idea that business has two aspects, the industrial and the
financial, and that (except in banking and the business
of finance) the two present alternative views of each fact.
In studying a particular business, that of a spinning-mill
or a foundry, you might study it from its books in terms
of sales and purchases, contracts and prices, or you
might study it in the operations of labour and machinery
upon the raw material in the various processes and the
changes in nature or position of forms of wealth.

Either study would yield a clear and complete knowledge of the structure and working of the business, but
from a different standpoint. The great mass of those
who are employed in the works or in the counting-office
are acquainted with only one of the aspects, and do not
require to know the other.

§ 2. *What Takes Place when Prices Fall?*

The manager alone is fully cognisant òf both aspects
of the business and is concerned with their inter-relations.
Looking at the business as a going concern, the book-
keeping side seems simply to follow and to register in
figures and names the facts of purchase, work, and sale,
and to constitute the industrial side. The relations between
the two sides are focussed in the will of the manager.

8

It is the business manager who directly determines to reduce the employment of capital and labour in a period of depression, and the conjoined action of business managers thus causes "unemployment." But what drives managers to this resolve? Does the real impulse come from the financial or from the industrial side? The immediate force which operates on managers dictating this policy is "falling prices." When "general prices" fall below a certain point, they make it "not worth while to go on producing" and production is checked with the result of "unemployment."

It is then to the phenomenon of "falling prices" we must turn. Prices are the real link of connection between the industrial and the financial side of a business. At first sight this will seem an admission of the dominance of finance, for we associate prices more closely with the money-medium than with the articles which are the objects of exchange. But when we definitely face the crucial question, How is a price-change brought about? we shall find that the directly operative force belongs to the industrial, not to the financial side. It proceeds from an alteration in the relation between the quantity of production and the quantity of sales effected in a given time. If production increases while there is no increase on the side of sales, the congestion of goods weighs down price as surely as if the operation were of the nature of a mechanical balance. On the other hand if production remains the same or is reduced, while the number of sales effected in a given time is larger than before, a rise of prices is effected. No seller and no trade reduces prices so long as it is possible to sell all that can be supplied at former prices. The only possible immediate cause of a fall of prices is an actual increase of supply in its relation to quantity demanded. It is of real importance to recognise that an actual over-stock is necessary to bring about a fall of prices, and that nothing else can bring it about.

This changed relation of Supply and Demand exhibited in an over-stock may not be considerable and may involve no great or lasting waste, but it must exist or be believed to exist. When therefore we are told that such and such political, industrial, financial facts, a rumour of war, a protective tariff, an influx of gold have brought about a "fall of prices," we know that these forces lie outside the direct line of action and can only affect prices by either increasing supply or by reducing demand. So when monetary authorities tell us that the great fall of wholesale prices since 1873 is due to matters affecting the supply of gold and silver money, we do right to insist on being shown precisely how the alleged deficiency in quantity of money has affected the quantitative relation between supply and demand for goods so as to reduce the proportion which the latter holds to the former.

§ 3. *Illicit Jumps in Monetary Explanations of "Depression."*

The connection between money and price in discussions of commercial crises and depressions is generally made by a process of illicit jumps. Somehow or other, we are told, an increased quantity of "money" will form a basis of improved credit and with the improved credit commercial confidence will revive, confidence will establish enterprise and general activity affording increased employment of capital and labour, and higher prices will ensue.

The exact point of connection between the mental or subjective phenomena called confidence and enterprise and the objective commercial facts of an increase of sales is always concealed. Bimetallists commonly assume that an increased quantity of money must cause a corresponding rise of prices, without taking the least trouble to show how this increase of money will necessarily induce purchasers of goods to increase the quantity of their purchases. I am not here concerned to deny that it will have this result, but it is clearly their business to prove it.

An increase of money which was privately hoarded by its possessors could manifestly have no effect on prices. If it was hoarded in banks, it could only operate by reducing the rate of discount, thus stimulating the purchases of those who borrow to buy.

The supposition that increased volume of money would of necessity either directly or by enlarged credit imply an increase of purchases corresponding to its size is unwarranted.

§ 4. Bimetallism can only Raise Prices by Raising Consumption.

It is, however, quite needless to open the whole currency question or to propound a theory of the extent of the influence of quantity of money upon prices. It suffices to affirm the principle that whatever influence an increase of money would exercise on prices must come by raising the quantity of purchases relative to the supply of articles offered for sale. It is essential to recognise that if bimetallism or any other monetary "ism" operates so as to stimulate increased production *equally* with consumption it can have no possible effect in raising general prices. For, if the result of a free flow of money is to bring about an increase of supply and a merely equivalent increase of quantity demanded (effective demand) prices must remain as before. If it be alleged that in commerce buyers only buy to sell, and that producers who obtained use of a freer and cheaper supply of money would only use it to increase their rate of production and swell the total of supply, the answer is that such use of the enhanced supply of money could have no possible influence in raising prices. Only that portion of the increased supply of money used by consumers of commodities in enhanced consumption would operate by changing the quantitative relation between the aggregate Supply and the aggregate Demand, and thus raise prices. Therefore, in order to make good their claim that a bimetallic coinage would raise prices, the advocates of this system must show that it would induce consumers to spend an increased proportion of their incomes in a demand for commodities. This I need hardly say they make no pretence to do. If they did show this result, it would be tantamount to admitting the previous existence of an excessive quantity of producing-power, *i.e.*, a condition of under-consumption. In other words, the view which finds in the state of currency the cause and the cure of depressed trade and prices can establish its position in no other wise than by admitting the accuracy of the analysis which refers the depression to under-consumption. If bimetallists actually claimed that their system of currency would maintain the full and economic adjustment between producing-power and consumption by stimulating the latter, it might be necessary to consider more closely the nature of their cure. But since they make no such claim no such necessity emerges.

§ 5. *Does a Fall of Prices Come from Increased Supply or Restricted Demand?*

Since a continuous fall of prices means nothing else than an actual excess of supply over quantity demanded at former prices, it may be explained either by the operation of forces which feed Supply without stimulating Demand to a corresponding extent, or by the operation of forces which act primarily as a restriction of demand. Since bimetallists repudiate the explanation that the fall of prices since 1873 is due to a cheapening of "cost" of production which has enlarged supply, they are driven to the alternative admission that the result of an insufficient supply of money is to restrict demand for goods. This admission is seldom made in so many words because currency men often seem to lose sight of the principle that price-change always means in the first instance a change in the quantitative relation of supply and quantity demanded at a former price. But the bimetallist position clearly rests upon the assumption that an insufficient supply of money disables purchasers from buying as much as they would otherwise have done. The two explanations of falling prices, an enlargement of supply and a restriction of demand, form, it is true, no logical antinomy; both forces may be operative in different degrees; but for testing the truth or falsehood of the financial explanation of depressed trade, we may treat them as alternatives. Our position is that the forces which depress prices have in fact operated by enabling larger quantities of goods to be added to supply at less labour-cost, and that in order to effect sales the owners of these goods have been constantly obliged to lower prices.

§ 6. *The Test of Sauerbeck's Index Numbers.*

Of the accuracy of this explanation Sauerbeck's tables seem to furnish a tolerably simple test. If diminished cost of production is the ultimate cause of falling prices we shall expect the prices of different goods to fall in different proportions, since the diminution of cost will differ in each case.

If on the other hand volume of money is the ultimate cause of falling prices we shall expect a corresponding fall in all prices. What do we actually find?

SAUERBECK'S INDEX NUMBERS.

Year.	Veg. Food.	Animal Food.	Sugar, Coffee, Tea.	Total Food.	Minerals.	Textiles.	Sundry Materials.	Total Materials.	Grand Total.
1873	106	109	106	107	141	103	106	114	111
1874	105	103	105	104	116	92	96	100	102
1875	93	108	100	100	101	88	92	93	96
1876	92	108	98	99	90	85	95	91	95
1877	100	101	103	101	84	85	94	89	94
1878	95	101	90	96	74	78	88	81	87
1879	87	94	87	90	73	74	85	78	83
1880	89	101	88	94	79	81	89	84	88
1881	84	101	84	91	77	77	86	80	85
1882	84	104	76	89	79	73	85	80	84
1883	82	103	77	89	76	70	84	77	82
1884	71	97	63	79	68	68	81	73	76
1885	68	88	63	74	66	65	76	70	72
1886	65	87	60	72	67	63	69	67	69
1887	64	79	67	70	69	65	67	67	68
1888	67	82	65	72	78	64	67	69	70
1889	65	86	75	75	75	70	68	70	72
1890	65	82	70	73	80	66	69	71	72
1891	75	81	71	76	76	59	69	68	72
1892	65	84	69	71	71	57	67	65	68
1893	59	85	75	68	68	59	68	65	68
1894	55	80	65	64	64	58	64	60	63

Not only do we find each group of commodities widely and variously differing from the others in the proportionate fall of price between 1873 and 1894, but there is no such general regularity in these fluctuations throughout the period as would seem necessary, were these changes all dominated by the single factor volume of currency. Moreover, if we analyse the several groups we see every possible variety of price-change in the different component articles consistent with a general downward tendency. The more we split up the groups into their component parts the larger and the more various the fluctuations in price. While this is inconsistent with an explanation of fall of prices by volume of currency it is not merely consistent with but would inevitably follow from the attribution of price-change to increase of supply stimulated by improvements of machinery of manufacture and transport and other reductions in the "cost" of production of a number of different commodities.

§ 7. *Want of "Confidence" not a Vera Causa— Itself a Symptom.*

The refusal of bimetallists and other monetary specialists to admit these tests arises from their refusal to realise the necessity of explaining price-change by facts relating to quantity of supply and demand of commodities other than money.

Rejecting on *a priori* grounds the idea of a general excess of production, they are driven to explain bad trade and the apparent surplus of forms of capital by causes affecting the quantity of money which operates upon public confidence. This attitude of mind is best illustrated in one who was in no sense a monetary specialist. The words in which J. S. Mill sums up his explanation of the periods when "commodities in general became unsaleable," producing a temporary condition of "general over-supply" form a most succinct expression of the fallacy. "The essentials of the doctrine are preserved when it is admitted that there cannot be permanent excess of production or of accumulation, though it be at the same time admitted that as there may be a temporary excess of any one article considered separately, so may there of commodities generally, not in consequence of over-production, but of a want of commercial confidence." *

Here we have the explicit explanation of a purely objective phenomenon, an excess of unsaleable articles, by reference to what is properly and primarily a purely subjective phenomenon, want of confidence. Want of commercial confidence can no more be a cause of an accumulation of unsaleable goods than a rise in the thermometer can be a cause of sunshine. Want of commercial confidence arises from the collapse of some businesses through inability to affect sales at profitable prices, the general decline of business profits arising from low prices, and a general lack of safe and profitable fields of investment. This prevalence of low prices simply registers the existence of an excess of supply over quantity demanded. Want of confidence then is nothing but a subjective interpretation of the already existing fact of a general excess of forms of capital, or productive power. It may be a convenient term to describe the attitude of mind of those who have money to invest and who refuse to place it, but it can

* "Unsettled Questions of Political Economy," p. 74.

furnish no explanation of the congested state of industry implied by the fact of general over-supply.

§ 8.   *The Notion that Reduced Cost of Production cannot Reduce all Prices, Disproved.*

One other deep-rooted fallacy underlies the currency explanation of the fall of prices, the *a priori* denial that a lowering of "cost of production" of all commodities can be a true cause of a fall of prices. Mill gave distinct utterance to this doctrine by arguing that, since all trade is exchange of commodities for commodities, any increase of supply must involve a corresponding increase of demand, so that each unit of the increased supply must exchange on the same terms, as before, even if the increased supply was due to reduced labour-cost of producing a unit of supply. But this argument rests on the assumption that everything which can be "demanded" will be "demanded," *i.e.*, that all producing-power is necessarily utilised in demand.

This doctrine has been lately reaffirmed by Dr. Smart in terms which seem to clearly expose the error which it contains. A general fall in cost of production would not, he maintains, in itself tend to a general fall of prices, for " if a particular trade were to take full advantage of the reduction of machinery by laying down proportionally more plant and extending production, the total cost would not diminish although the cost per item would. In such circumstances, however, this trade could maintain the exchange value of its commodities per item only if demand increased *pari passu* with the increase of supply. And *demand would increase*—assuming equal elasticity—if the production of all the other goods increased in the same ratio." *   Now the

* "Studies in Economics", p. 175.

assumption that demand *would* increase is without warrant. Dr. Smart is only justified in assuming that demand *might* increase. All increase of supply *might* be demanded and consumed as fast as it grew. If that actually occurred there would be no alteration in the quantitative relation of supply and demand (quantity demanded) at the different stages of industry. Moreover, there could then be no fall of prices. Dr. Smart thinks that scarcity of money causes the general fall of prices which others have attributed to reduced cost of production. But if every increase of supply was taken off in increased demand, no scarcity of money (assuming there were such a thing) could affect prices. This may be tested by a closer attention to any class of prices. Suppose a general increase of supply in all retail shops and a corresponding increase of demand as a necessary counterpart, retailers would not lower prices but would sell the increased quantity of goods at the same prices as before. If scarcity of money is to be operative in reducing prices, it can only be by preventing demand from keeping pace with increased supply, *i.e.*, by defeating the operation of what has just been assumed as a necessary law, the effective demand of the whole of supply.

It is of course true that with every increase of supply an increase of "purchasing power" or possible demand is created. If this power is exercised, nothing that happens to the supply of money can prevent prices from standing firm. If scarcity of money does operate on prices it can only be by preventing some of the possible demand from becoming effective. If prices do fall it means that those who have the power to demand all the increased supply, do not exercise it, but withhold it.

§ 9.   The Right Place of "Money" as an Agent in Falls of Prices.

It may be important to ascertain how far scarcity of money may be the cause which induces some owners of demand-power to withhold that power. This, I think, is the point where monetary influences act. If all exchange were of commodities with commodities direct, it is clear there could be no over-supply and that the alleged power of supply to create a corresponding effective demand would be always valid. The possibility of withholding Demand only arrives with the use of some forms of money, by the ownership of which power to demand may be held in solution as a lien upon the future. In other words the use of money is a necessary condition to that failure of demand to keep full pace with the growth of supply which is expressed in a fall of prices. But no proof is forthcoming that there is in fact anything which can be rightly called "scarcity" of money, or how such "scarcity" increases the tendency of owners of demand-power to withhold that power.

Money is indeed the social instrument by which over-saving or under-consumption becomes possible. By means of money the refusal to consume may be practised to an excess for certain long periods of time. But this excess is not shown to vary with quantity of money in a community.

Over-saving from the social standpoint is seen to arise from the effort of a number of individuals to postpone a larger quantity of their power to demand commodities than is socially useful in maintaining forms of capital. This refusal is quite consistent with the amplest supply of money, and wherever it occurs prices must fall. Close analysis shows over-saving or under-consumption as the only immediate cause of a general fall of prices: scarcity of money is not proved to be either directly or indirectly a *vera causa*.

CHAPTER VIII

PALLIATIVES OF UNEMPLOYMENT

§ 1. A Test for Palliatives. Do they Raise Consumption?

IF under-consumption, chiefly due to excessive attempts to capitalise unearned elements of individual income, is the direct cause of the mass of unemployment, no remedy will be effective which does not help to raise the general standard of consumption. The radical and permanent remedies will lie in the lines of that progressive movement outlined in the last chapter. But our analysis must also furnish a test which is applicable to the numerous proposals which seek by special measures to cure or to alleviate the malady of unemployment.

It is quite beyond the scope of this enquiry to examine or even to describe most of these proposals. But some short summary under several heads may be of service in order that we may ascertain how far they satisfy the essential economic test.

§ 2. Labour Bureaux as Clearing-Houses.

At the threshold lies the proposal for the establishment

of a system of Labour Bureaux as a department of the public service, which shall register the names and require-ments of workers who seek employment, and of employers offering· employment, and shall assist to place the two bodies in communication with one another. An effective organisation of this sort would reduce to a minimum those elements of "waste" arising from leakage between jobs to which lowly organised trades are specially prone, and would impart some increased elasticity to industry by enabling employers to execute their new designs with less trouble and less loss of time than is imposed by the present need of seeking for suitable labour. Workers out of employment who possessed some labour-power for which there was a growing demand would be able to utilise it more speedily and more advantageously than at present. Labour Bureaux would thus impart increased fluidity to labour and would for the lower-organised trades undertake some of the important functions of the Trade Union in the skilled and well-organised trades. If Labour Bureaux under local management and ordered on the same general principles were kept in close and constant relation with each` other, a Clearing House system for Labour might be established which would reduce to a minimum the waste arising from leakages and minor trade displacements. At the same time, though such work would be conducive to industrial order and might help to throw light upon the extent and nature of fluctuations in employment, no system of Labour Bureaux would materially assist to solve the problem of the un-employed. The ability to fill gaps in employment some-what more easily will not considerably increase the net quantity of employment. Even when Labour Bureaux have found temporary employment for a considerable proportion of their applicants, we are not entitled to assume that the net amount of employment in the community has been increased: for it may be the case that the selection of employees recommended by the Labour Bureaux has involved the rejection or the non-selection of others who remain unemployed. In trades where there exists normally an over-supply of labour it is difficult to admit that the establishment of increased facilities for hiring labour will increase the number of those employed, though it might allow a more discriminative process of selection.

Even if we assume that a certain quantity of productive work remained undone at present because of the lack of a system placing employers in close communication with employees, this admission only implies that Labour Bureaux might somewhat increase the available power of production. But in periods of depressed trade, and in many trades normally, there exists an excessive power of production, and the addition made to production by Labour Bureaux would not be economically valid unless it could be shown that a corresponding rise in consumption was involved. In a town where more houses are being built than can find occupants, no net continuous increase of employment would be caused by a Labour Bureau which enabled builders to secure an easier supply of all necessary labour and so to put up houses faster than before, and if this same condition held in all or most towns no system of mere labour-exchange, however well-conducted, would increase the total quantity of employment over a long area of time. Even the stoppage of waste from "leakages" and misplacements would only be of real assistance in a community where there exists no general over-supply of productive power.

§ 3. *The Elimination of Minor Forms of Waste.*

In order that Labour Bureaux may successfully operate as Clearing Houses it is of course essential that they should possess the confidence alike of genuine working-men and of employers. Arising in many cases in connection with Relief Work they have remained on ? semi-philanthropic or charitable footing, failing to draw or to deserve the application of employers in search of the best available labour, and also failing to induce skilled and capable workers to have regular recourse to them as a means of getting good and remunerative employment. Whether the Labour Bureau should itself undertake to ascertain the industrial character and qualifications of applicants, confining itself to the register of sound cases, or whether it should pursue the general policy of registering all comers, is a disputed point. The difficulties attending character-enquiry and the distrust it not unnaturally engenders seem to favour the perfectly free register, though every facility might be afforded for the collection and communication of such information as would enable both parties to a bargain to understand the nature of the contract upon which they entered. If the Labour Bureau were in every centre of population recognised as an important public institution conducted on sound business principles, it would probably gain the confidence of all classes of employers and workers who were in need of each other and found the ordinary private modes of meeting inadequate.

The Labour Bureau might of course with great advan-

9

tage combine with such work other important functions, especially the ascertainment and publication of reliable statistics relating to all forms of local industries. But the relief work of a charitable or semi-charitable kind which is often done by Labour Bureaux must be left to other public or private agencies, if the Bureaux are to perform effectively the work of Labour Exchanges.

In relation to the "Unemployed" the Labour Bureaux would rank as one of the many means of increasing the productive efficiency of the community by eliminating certain forms of waste. Where the progress of Consumption is such as to fully utilise every increase of productive power the full advantage of this labour-saving system is obtained: in a condition of industry where the labour-market is in general over-stocked the net gain of this and similar forms of economy is reduced to a minimum.

§ 4. Schemes for Increasing Employment.

The different schemes the object of which is to give increased quantity of employment might be classified in various ways, according to the kind of work which they seek to provide, skilled or unskilled, agricultural or manu-facturing; according to the kind of unemployment they seek to alleviate, casual, season, or permanent; according as they adopt voluntary or compulsory methods, State or private enterprise; according as they seek to enlarge present modes of employment or to create new ones; according as they are generally educative or purely industrial in their motives.

The most convenient classification for our purpose is that which distinguishes the various proposals according as they are intended to relieve:

(α) The chronic glut of low-skilled labour in towns or flowing into towns.

(β) Temporary unemployment due to season or trade fluctuations.

§ 5. Labour Colonies—Penal Conditions.

Under the first head we may properly treat the proposals for the establishment of farm colonies and other labour colonies. Various colonies of different types where the labour is chiefly employed in cultivation of the land exist already in England or on the continent, and a wider application of the various systems is often advocated. These colonies may be divided into several classes.*

Several penal colonies for convicted beggars and loafers exist in Belgium and Holland, where some thousands of men are employed in agricultural work under a kind of military discipline. These institutions stand in organisation somewhere between the laxer workhouse and the prison, but differ essentially from both in that the educating and reforming influences are more dominant. An attempt is made to give a sound moral and industrial basis to broken-down characters. The minority of the Labour Commission in their Report urge the establishment of this order of labour colonies in England.

"For the invalids of labour, those unfortunates who have already become unfit for regular work, we should welcome the establishment of experimental labour colonies, under strict government, to which any man might be committed for a fixed term, to undergo the course of mental and

* For this division and much information bearing on these colonies I am indebted to a valuable paper by Mr. Herbert Samuel, entitled "A Survey of the Unemployed Problem."

technical educational discipline most calculated to restore him to the ranks of the workers." For dealing with the "sturdy beggar" and the professional tramps such methods mark a distinct advance upon the present system of mendicancy tempered by the casual ward, and careful experiments upon these lines merit serious attention. In so far as the tramp and able-bodied pauper classes are constantly fed by the off-scourings of the lower-skilled labour market all attempts to deal with them touch the subject of "the unemployed," but since these people can hardly be ranked among the occupied classes, their treatment must be regarded more as a palliative of a special symptom of the disease than as a direct and effective treatment of the disease itself. Though it is plainly desirable that society should be relieved as far as possible from the contamination of a parasitic tramp population, public work given upon penal terms to such people cannot be looked upon as a direct or important contribution to the solution of the unemployed problem, so long as nothing is done to obviate those defects of low-skilled employment which help to produce the tramp and the sturdy rogue.

§ 6. Farm Colonies for Paupers.

If such colonies are regarded as a possible development of a more humanised and rational penal code, administered by the Home Office as part of our Reformatory System, other colonies not dissimilar in administration and in methods might grow from a specialisation of the Poor Law work. Some agricultural labour, though not of a very remunerative sort, is carried on by Boards of Guardians in gardens and small farms for the supply of vegetables and other food to the workhouse, and a separate establishment to which select pauper labour might be drafted, and where removed from the benumbing influence of the ordinary workhouse it might be more productively utilised and trained towards efficiency and independence, is no unreasonable development of an enlightened Poor Law. It may be remembered that for such a step no revolutionary legislation is required. The Guardians have power already under Statutes of George III. and William IV. to obtain and occupy fifty acres of land in each parish of their union for the purpose of providing work. They are able to take action as soon as the Local Government Board issues rules for their guidance, and several Unions have the projected experiment under consideration.

Moreover it is open for philanthropic enterprise to undertake this work where Boards of Guardians are unwilling to incur the expense of an experiment on their own account. Boards are already empowered by the Local Government Board to send able-bodied men to privately organised Farm Colonies where they will receive training in work, and to pay 5/- a week out of the rates for the maintenance of each man so sent. Both the Hadleigh Colony and Mr. Hazell have received paupers upon these terms for work and training on their farms.

§ 7. Mr. Charles Booth's Suggested Labour Colonies for Class B.

These schemes though well deserving of attention upon grounds of humanity do little more than touch the fringe of the "unemployed" question. They belong rather to the important subject of the humanisation of our criminal and poor law systems. By removing a certain number of industrial weaklings from the free industrial society which they burden and contaminate, and by ordering their lives for them with some regard to comfort, education, and self-respect, a grievous stain upon our civilisation might be obliterated. It is, however, improbable that any considerable number of these weaklings can be converted into self-dependent members of society, and it must be remembered that if turned again upon the low-skilled labour-market with whatever fair equipment of efficiency, they go to swell a glut and can only get work by keeping others out.

The unemployed question cannot be solved or its pressure materially abated by taking the most inefficient members of the lowest classes (Mr. Booth's Classes A and B) and converting them into members of Classes C or even D. The permanent plethora of inefficient and even of fairly efficient low-skilled labour must not be shirked. It forms a terrible centre-piece of the unemployed problem and challenges "heroic" remedies. Mr. Charles Booth perceiving how these classes are overstocked, suggests the possibility of a wider system of labour colonies than any yet in operation. His guarded and tentative proposal is for a large social drainage scheme which might remove the whole or the greater part of the irregular, inefficient, low-paid labour included under his Class B with the families dependent upon them.

"Put practically, but shortly, my idea is that these people should be allowed to live as families in industrial groups, planted wherever land and building materials were cheap; being well housed, well fed, and well warmed; and taught, trained, and employed from morning to night on work, indoors or out, for themselves or on Government account; in the building of their own dwellings, or the cultivation of the land, in the making of clothes, or in the making of furniture. That in exchange for the work done the Government should supply materials and whatever else was needed. On this footing it is probable that the State would find the work done very dear and by so much would lose. How much the loss would be could only be told by trying the system experimentally. There would be no competition with the outside world. It would be merely that the State, having these people on its hands, obtained whatever value it could out of their work. They would become servants of the State. Accounts would have to be kept, however, and for this purpose the work done would have to be priced at the market rate. It would even be well that wages should be charged and credited, each person at the fair proportionate rate, so that the working of one community might be compared with another, and the earnings of one man or one family with others in the same community. The deficiency could then be allotted in the accounts proportionately to each, or if the State made no claim for interest or management, there might be a surplus to allot, opening out a road back to the outside world. It would, moreover, be necessary to set a limit to the current deficiency submitted to by the State, and when the account of any family reached this point, to move them on to the poor-house where they would live as a family no longer." *

* "Life and Labour of the People," vol. I, p. 167.

§ 8. Practical Difficulties of "Social Drainage."

Such a proposal differs radically from the penal or pauper colonies in two ways, first because it assumes the voluntary presence of the members of a colony and therefore dispenses with the severe disciplinary methods needed where the draft to the colony is compulsory, secondly because it preserves the family as the social unit and endeavours to secure the continuance of the motives which operate in a free community so far as is consistent with the conditions of the experiment. .

The difficulties which the large effective application of such a scheme would involve are very great, perhaps insuperable in such a country as England. The chief of these difficulties would be:

1. The unwillingness of city families of the "very poor" to leave the customary slum environment and to undertake a more orderly life necessitating any degree of regularity of work.

2. The inability of the members of such a community to submit to the most humane and thoughtful discipline required to keep the "colonies" from contact with the outside world. The population of such volunteer colonies would be constantly shifting.

3. The expense to the public purse which would of course be much greater where whole families are maintained than upon colonies for single men, and which would be enhanced by the "shifting" character of the population and the consequent ineffectiveness of the labour that was done.

The voluntary basis of such colonies would in effect be a far more fatal obstacle than the public expense when we take into due consideration the enormous cost, direct and indirect, which society incurs in keeping this class under present circumstances. But apart from these practical suggestions the scheme is economically sound, that is to say, if such communities could be maintained upon the basis described we should at one and the same time derive two great benefits, the humane care and a decent standard of material comfort for the class which is unable to look after itself, and a distinct relief from the glut of low-skilled inefficient labour which would considerably strengthen the industrial and social position of those working classes which stand just above the class that was removed.

§ 9. German and Dutch Free Labour Colonies.

I am not aware that any adequate experiment upon Mr. Booth's basis has been tried. The labour colonies open to all comers are in most cases confined to single men, and for the most part are destined as temporary shelters and training schools, not as permanent institutions for relieving the pressure of the labour-market. Of such a character are the twenty-six German Labour Colonies, which though nominally open to all comers are practically shunned by the great mass of *bonâ fide* working men and are chiefly utilised by ex-criminals who number no less than 76 per cent. of the population of these colonies. About one half of the colonists seek temporary relief, the rest loaf round from colony to colony. The general economic effect of these colonies is almost nil. The colonies do not interfere with the labour-market, because they do not deal with the problem of the want of employment of the respectable workman." *

* "Report on the Unemployed (1893)", p. 287.

The Dutch Free Labour Colonies at Frederiksoord, Wilhelmsoord, and Wilhelminaasoord conform more closely to the proposal of Mr. Booth in that they recognise the family and provide a permanent house for the colonists, educating the children. Though agriculture is the chief occupation a number of subsidiary industries are attached, such as Matmaking, Blacksmithy, Tailoring, Carpentry, Brickmaking, Basketmaking and Furniture making. The success of the Dutch colonies is not, however, such as to afford great encouragement to the advocates of labour colonies. The population is somewhat smaller than in 1873, though the tendency towards large families of children, many of whom return to the colony after they are launched in the outside world, seems to point to the danger of breeding a permanent race of paupers, as one which would deserve the most serious consideration in the wider application of such a system. The average annual cost of a family to the Dutch charitable public appears to amount to about £23 per annum, inclusive of interest on the capital invested in land and plant.

§ 10.   The Starnthwaite Experiment.

So far as effective labour and any definite improvement in industrial character and position are concerned we can scarcely look with any degree of hope to colonies which are open to all comers, exercising no selection. In England at any rate the most hopeful experiments would seem to be those which selected their material from the low-skilled labour which is displaced from agricultural work or which is already deposited in town life. Among those which are now on foot the experiment of the Home Colonisation Society at Starnthwaite in Westmoreland is, in its economic structure and object, of the highest interest. While admitting women and recognising the family life, it exercises a certain selection of colonists and is animated by the idea of so organising groups of labourers who would otherwise be competing for employment in an overcrowded market, that they may be able, with some outside assistance of capital, to apply their labour so as to make a self-supporting community. The colony, however, is at present in a tentative condition, having been considerably crippled in its earlier development by difficulties of management, and its numbers hitherto have been too small to test how far its design of being self-supporting is feasible. The idea which it embodies, that of a permanent settlement of selected working-class families grouped in a self-sufficing and co-operative community, relieves the Starnthwaite colony from many of the objections which apply to the free temporary relief colonies, and if the permanence and co-operative spirit can be maintained upon a larger basis of population it should afford a very valuable lesson.

§ 11. *Educative Colonies at Hadleigh and Elsewhere.*

The largest example of a Labour Colony, or more strictly a group of labour colonies, directly designed for dealing with the unemployed, is that undertaken by the Salvation Army. The work both in the Elevator Workshops and in the Farm Colony at Hadleigh, is upon the individual as distinct from the family basis and is confined to single male applicants. In the employment at the Workshops there is no real selection upon entry, all may be admitted who have registered themselves at the Labour Bureau and are unable to get outside places, though men once admitted are required to satisfy a certain test of work as a condition of remaining. Apart from bridging over a certain period of distress, the chief use of the Workshop is in enabling a selection to be made of men who are suitable for drafting on to the Farm Colony, with a view to a sounder and fuller industrial training, chiefly in connection with agriculture. The workshops thus act for the main as a relief agency, the greater part of those resident at any given time being reabsorbed into the class of casual workers. Out of those who volunteer for the Hadleigh Farm a certain number are selected and the farm authorities make a final choice out of these. A certain number also enter without passing through the Elevator Workshop. It is very difficult to estimate the success of this experiment. In the earlier years (1891 to 1893) the bulk of the colonists were engaged in non-agricultural work, in brickfields, in making a wharf and embankments, or in manufacturing work. Since 1893 more attention has been paid to the agricultural side with a considerable reduction in the net cost of the colony.

Valuable educative and restorative work has doubtless been done, though the full work of the colony cannot be ascertained until the Over Sea Colony which it was designed to feed with labour has been put into operation. At present only a minority of the colonists remain for any considerable time, so that the colony .cannot be regarded as an important part of the social drainage system.

The smaller but more carefully ordered training farm established by Mr. Hazell in connection with the Self-Help Emigration Society proves pretty conclusively that unskilled men, even when carefully selected, cannot be trained for farm work except at a very considerable cost, though a satisfactory number of those emigrated appear to have made a successful start in the New World.

The reports of two continental colonies designed to train and utilise the labour of selected able-bodied men, one at Wortel in Belgium, the other at La Chalmelle near Paris, seem to point to the same conclusion, that such colonies cannot be maintained except at considerable expense.

§ 12. Mr. Mather's Scheme of Training and Agricultural Colonies.

If it is once clearly recognised that all present evidence tends to the conclusion that neither open colonies nor selected colonies for training or for productive work can be made self-supporting, or nearly so, the public will be in a position to judge of the utility of this mode of dealing with "the unemployed." Unfortunately even social reformers so competent as Mr. Mather, whose scheme is distinctly the most statesmanlike of those yet conceived, linger under the impression that "it is necessary to recognise the fact that the labour of any able-bodied man upon land, can, under proper directions and conditions, be of at least an equal value to the cost of his maintenance." Mr. Mather's scheme of Farm Training Colonies is . briefly this: County Councils with money advanced by the State are to acquire land in each county suitable for Training Colonies, and to erect buildings to accommodate as many men as can be supported on the land, single men or married couples. The staple work is to be agricultural, partly in reclaiming land capable of cultivation when reclaimed, partly in the utilisation of good land by manual labour for arable-dairying, and other cropping, for which manual labour is largely available. Auxiliary industries which require small capital and can be carried on by intermittent labour are to be attached as a means of utilising that part of the working time which cannot be occupied upon the land. To such a colony the Poor Law Authorities should send men of the "unemployed" class who seek relief through employment only and who have not hitherto been in receipt of Poor Law relief. While the colony is to be managed by the County Council, the deficit, if any, is to be borne by the Poor Law Authorities.

"The advantages of this system of dealing with the well-conducted members of the unemployed working classes would be threefold. In the first place the money earned would come largely out of the land which the labour of the men had rendered more productive, thus adding to the material wealth without detracting from the productive labour of any other individual in the nation. Secondly, the man and his family would be wholly or almost entirely sustained by the work of his own hand. Thirdly, no taint of pauperism could attach to this system and no disfranchisement be connected therewith." *

For a comprehensive scheme upon these lines there is much to be said: the difficulties of administration by the County Council and of the relations which would subsist between the Local Government Board, the County Council, and the Poor Law Authorities, might quite conceivably be settled on a satisfactory basis of adjustment. But the financial results which Mr. Mather claims to be reasonably expected cannot for one moment be admitted. He pro-

* "Draft Scheme to provide Work for the Unemployed Working Classes," p. 5.

poses that the money advanced by the State should be
an investment upon which ordinary interest could be paid,
and he thinks that good management would enable the
County Council to dispense with aid from the Poor Law
Authorities in payment of deficits. Neither of these ex-
pectations could be fulfilled. The very name Training
Colony is sufficient to indicate that it cannot be self-
supporting. No educational work can be self-supporting.
The State would have to provide money for which it
would receive no direct financial return, each year the
Poor Law Authorities would have to pay a certain sum
for each man sent to the colony. Once recognise that
this investment of public money must look for its return
not in pecuniary interest but in certain unmeasurable
forms of public good, the improvement of the industrial
character of certain workers, the public guarantee of a
decent livelihood without degradation, a certain direct
relief of the low-skilled labour-market, and the proposal
takes a reasonable shape.

Some such scheme of Training Colonies (divorced, if
possible, from direct association with our Poor Law system)
involving a recognition of the public utility of guaran-
teeing work to all willing workers, and practical training
for work to all willing to be trained, is perhaps the
largest and the most serviceable of the palliatives for " the
unemployed."

§ 13. Economic Precautions required in Labour Colonies.

If such a scheme could in fact be worked on a self-
supporting basis no distinctively economic difficulty would
arise. But when it is recognised that these and all other

Labour Colonies will draw subsidies from public or private sources, one grave economic danger must be plainly confronted and met.

No produce of a Labour Colony should be placed on the open market in such a way as to compete with the produce of outside English labour. Such produce being subsidised will in the open market be able to undersell and to displace goods produced under ordinary commercial conditions. The result of such underselling will be to drive certain weaker outside businesses below the margin of subsistence and to deprive the workers formerly engaged in them of their employment. Thus the "employment" given at the public expense or by charity in a labour colony would cause an amount of unseen unemployment as large as that which it cured. This condition though commonly admitted in theory, is often ignored in practice. Since it is not possible for labour colonies to be fully self-supporting in the sense that they produce all they consume, it is necessary for them to purchase in the open market what they are unable to produce. To meet this expense they are often disposed to confine a large proportion of their capital and labour to producing those goods which they can make with the greatest advantage and to sell them in neighbouring markets. The result is they inevitably help to congest outside markets, lower prices, and drive the weakest outside producers from the field. Prison labour, workhouse labour, farm colony labour, must have this result. If Salvation Army matches and furniture, if Starnthwaite vegetables and fruit are placed upon the open markets of the neighbourhood, they cannot fail to exercise a force which makes for the "unemployment" of the least efficient outside competitors.

This argument is not really met by showing that a colony does not directly and consciously underbid: it helps to increase Supply, and any increase of Supply without a corresponding growth of Demand necessarily brings down prices. It may indeed be urged with some force that the effect produced upon prices and employment in these trades will be more than compensated for by the effect of the increased demand represented by the consumption of other outside goods purchased by the Colony. Set these two tendencies against one another, and the result will be a net increase of consumption, represented by the improved standard of consumption of the colonists, which will be reflected in a rise of aggregate employment for the whole community. This argument is sound, but it does not justify the retention of a practice which, inflicts upon certain special English industries the injury of an illegitimate competition. Most advocates of Colonies and other schemes of public employment endeavour to provide against this danger by confining the labour of colonists to the production of commodities which are either consumed on the colony, or which if placed upon the outside markets only compete with goods imported from foreign countries.

§ 14. Difficulties of Disposing of Surplus Produce.

A single colony, if it is to make an effective use of its land, its labour, and its location, must necessarily specialise its productive work so far as to produce larger quantities of certain agricultural and manufactured goods than its inhabitants require for their consumption. The difficulty of disposing of this surplus produce without inflicting injury upon outside producers might be minimised, if it were possible to establish a system of labour colonies, some engaged in rural occupations, others on co-operative town work. Even two well-ordered colonies, one in the town, another in the country, might effect an exchange of surplus produce upon such terms that everything which was produced could be consumed by the colonists. Although it is highly improbable that two or more such colonies of "unemployed" could form a wholly self-sufficient group, it seems quite possible that they might dispense with the necessity of an outside market for their goods, while the need under which they would lie of purchasing in the outside market certain articles for their own use, would of course be perfectly innocuous. The small experiments in Labour Colonies have never fairly tested the possibilities of effective co-operation, for the considerable deficit involved in their working is due chiefly to the necessity of purchasing in the outside market the bulk of the articles which they consume and the materials and tools for their work, an expense which might be largely reduced by the co-operation of a chain of labour colonies organised with the express design of mutual support for industrial life.

The dependence of England upon foreign countries for a large proportion of the agricultural produce she consumes, affords ample opportunities for the disposal of English farm produce by a displacement of imports. Our imports of agricultural produce for consumption amounted in 1894 to more than £115,000,000, of which corn and wheat exceeded £48,000,000, while the direct and indirect products of the dairy: butter, cheese, bacon, ham, lard, and milk cost £35,000,000, foreign eggs £3,750,000, fresh meat and vegetables over £5,000,000. It seems possible that labour farm colonies which could devote themselves to the production of these goods might place their subsidised produce on the English markets without the same direct injury which would result from placing manufactured goods on town markets. But even here it must not be forgotten that foreign agricultural produce would only be displaced by an underselling which would be likely to injure English producers of the same classes of articles. If subsidised labour colonies should displace Danish butter they would do so to the detriment of those English farmers who under present circumstances produce a large part of our butter supply. There are very few classes of produce, agricultural or other, which could be produced by a labour colony and which are at present exclusively in the hands of foreigners.

§ 15. Scheme of Afforestation.

These economic dangers and difficulties do not of course apply to schemes of agricultural improvement with or without State assistance which are conducted on purely *bonâ fide* business lines. Of such schemes the simplest and most entirely unobjectionable is that of Afforestation.

If the estimates of Dr. Slick and other authorities are correct, that England contains 8,000,000 acres well suited for the growth of timber, and that 6,000,000 of these would grow a quantity equal to our present imports, that the industry could be run upon an ordinary business basis and would provide employment for large quantities of unskilled labour during nearly the whole of the year, we have here a scheme which would satisfy every economic test. There is no economic reason why capital should not be advanced by the State for the establishment

10*

of such an industry, supposing it can be worked, as
Dr. Slick affirms, to yield a profit of 2¾ per cent. after
allowing for compound interest on the necessary outlay
during the long period that must elapse before returns
come in. Indeed it might be possible to go further· and
allow the legitimacy of a public outlay of capital without
interest, assuming that the timber grown displaced a trade
which was entirely of an import character. The large
employment of low-skilled labour in such a rural industry
might prove to be˙ the best occupation for subsidised
labour colonies, if it were deemed necessary to establish
them as a means of dealing with " the unemployed."

*§ 16.   Establishment of Small Holders as a Means
of Increased Agricultural Employment.*

Other proposals for a revival of English agriculture, by
the establishment of small holders with such a property
in the land they cultivate and such command of capital
as shall enable them to place dairy produce, fruit, vegetables,
pork and bacon, fowls and eggs upon the market at
profitable prices, are interesting contributions to the solution
of the unemployed problem, provided one point is kept
clearly in mind. Such schemes, if they are to contain
the elements of success, must not be primarily devoted
to the provision of work for those who are already
unemployed. Because there is unemployed labour and
vacant land it by no means follows that the planting of
this labour upon this land will be a serviceable mode of
dealing with unemployment. If bodies of trained, able-
bodied agriculturists with sufficient capital of their own,
or furnished by the public, can be put upon good land,
acquired without great expense or leased upon terms

which will evoke the application of the best energy of the occupiers, with ability to co-operate so far as to keep down certain expenses of production, of transport, and of sale, it seems quite possible that a greatly increased employment upon the land might be profitably found. It does not seem likely that those who are displaced from employment in the towns, or other town-bred persons, army pensioners, or the rank and file of the unemployed can be thus entrusted with the use of land and capital upon this business footing with any chance of success. But small farmers, picked agricultural labourers, country mechanics and others might succeed, provided they had security of their holdings upon reasonable terms and were possessed of sufficient capital, intelligence, and willingness to combine for certain common ends.

§ 17. An Illustration of Small Holding Scheme.

The following scheme of small farm settlements upon corporate tenancy, drafted by Mr. Mather, may be taken as illustrative of this line of progress:

"Every County Council should receive applications from those who seek to obtain a permanent living from the land. Landowners should be asked to send to the County Council particulars of any available farms which may be suitable for the purpose. On the general suitability of any farm being approved, the Council should convene a meeting of the applicants; and if the farm be accepted at such a meeting by a sufficient number to take up the entire area, the Council should appoint provisional Trustees or managers to act for the applicants. These Trustees should then arrange terms with the owner of the land, and settle its allotment and the buildings suitable for the

applicants. They should next submit to the County
Council full particulars of the terms which can be settled
with the owner of the land, the areas desired to be
taken by each of the intending occupiers, and the cost
of the buildings necessary. If the County Council approve
of the proposed terms, they should then recommend a
loan to be made by the State to the Trustees of the
sum necessary for the erection of the buildings and laying
out the property.

" On such a loan being sanctioned, the Trustees would
acquire the property and erect the buildings, and the
holdings would be allotted to the respective applicants.
Before possession was given, every applicant would have
to undertake to do, within six months of entry, the fencing
and certain other specified work, mainly in relation to
the out-buildings, which could reasonably be required to
be done by the occupier. He might then take possession
on any one of three different systems. He might (*a*)
sign an ordinary agreement of tenancy on terms agreed
upon with the Trustees; or (*b*) pay at least one-tenth
the cost of the buildings upon his holding, executing at
the same time a deed stating the amount remaining due
from him for the same, and the annual charge upon it,
calculated at 4 per cent. interest; or (*c*) agree to pay
annually 6 per cent. interest on the total cost for a term
of 25 years, which at the end of that term would dis-
charge his liability in respect of the buildings.

§ 18.   *Corporate Tenancy and other Co-operative Elements.*

Such schemes having for their primary object the
business aim of placing larger quantities of English agricul-

tural produce upon the market at the profitable rates, would exercise a certain curative influence upon the malady of unemployment. By affording increased employment on the land they would check the constant flow of rural labour to the towns, and would render far more effective than before the other remedies which might be ·applied to the direct relief of unemployment in the towns. But if these schemes of agricultural business are to succeed it is most important that they should be planned with a single view to the improvement of agriculture, and not directly with the object of "making employment on the land." This latter effect should be left to flow naturally from the attainment of the former. The best available labour should be put upon the best available land, with freedom of cultivation and a sufficiency of capital. A scheme like that of Corporate Tenancy involving as its foundation some mutual aid and confidence, would form a basis of co-operation in the use of machinery, dairy appliances, storehouses, which would develop naturally certain economies of transport and marketing, securing for the producers a large proportion of the profits which at present pass to collectors, carriers, salesmen, and other grades of middlemen. Last but not least such groups of small holders could by the development of Agricultural Credit Banks, secure for themselves that command of capital and flexibility of business outlay which is so essential to successful competition under the terms of modern industry.

§ *19. Economic Criticism.   National versus International Policy.*

In forming any general estimate of these proposals as

contributions to the solution of the Unemployed problem, we must keep in mind two economic points.

In the first place so far as these schemes of agricultural revival are directed to the increase of English industry by the displacement of foreign agricultural and other goods, they are purely national remedies. If by improved methods of dairy farming we can enable English butter to beat out of the market Danish and Brittany butter, we are simply increasing employment in England by diminishing employment in Denmark and Brittany, and the problem of unemployment merely shifts its locale, unless the producers in Denmark and Brittany can force a new market either at home or elsewhere for their butter at a reduced price. The objection which is sometimes urged to the effect that the displacement of any class of imports will throw out of employment the capital and labour engaged in those English manufactures which produce export goods to pay for the imports, has no validity. If English agriculturists increase their production by the amount which was formerly imported, they will be able to get in exchange and consume those manufactured goods which formerly went out in export trade, or their equivalents. But when due regard is paid to the rapidly growing importance of the international aspect of all industrial questions, it is not possible to contemplate as a final and satisfactory solution of "unemployment" an improvement of English agricultural production which merely enables England to oust a foreign competitor, and to secure for herself a larger share of the same aggregate of agricultural employment. If this argument seems to any a begging of the question, I would refer them to the general analysis of unemployment for a recognition of the fact that an increased production has no necessary force which can stimulate a corresponding increase of consumption. It might therefore not improbably happen that an improvement of English agriculture would give increased employment upon English soil, and might be attended by a reduced employment in Denmark or elsewhere. There will be no rise of aggregate employment in the larger industrial community to which both England and Denmark belong, unless it can be shown that the result of English improvements has been to raise the aggregate of consumption in this larger community, and this is not shown by proving that more is consumed in England unless it can also be proved that less is not consumed in Denmark.

While such a consideration need not deter us from any measures of agricultural improvement in England, we should recognise that the ever closening international relations will prevent us from holding the full advantages from such improvements, unless the supreme test of a rise in the level of consumption over the whole competing area is satisfied.

§ 20. *The Gain of Agricultural Revival should go Chiefly to Labour.*

The second point is this. In regarding the influence of schemes of agricultural revival upon the volume of employment, it is essential that the chief gain of such revival should pass to wages of labour and not to profits and rents of the landowning and large capitalist classes. For we have observed that whereas increased wages will for the most part be " consumed " in raising the standard of comfort for agricultural workers, increased rents and profits will to

a large extent be "saved" and invested or banked, so
as to increase the excess of producing-power in forms of
capital, and to maintain and aggravate the general in-
stability of trade. Schemes for increased production, even
while they seem to employ more labour and capital, will
in large measure defeat their end unless an increased
proportion of the enlarged consuming-power which they
generate passes to those who will use it in steady demand
for commodities.

§ 21.   *Proposal of Secondary or Alternative Trades.*

It is not within the scope of this work to attempt a
description of the various proposals to deal with temporary
unemployment of skilled and unskilled workers due to
"seasonal" or "trade fluctuations." A brief application
of one economic test to the more general palliatives must
suffice.

It is often suggested that if season workers, such as
house painters and other members of the building trades,
were possessed of a second or alternative trade which they
could ply during the winter, their economic position would
be greatly strengthened. It is natural that those who
look at the single trade should take this view. Many go
so far as to regard it as a chief function of a Technical
Education System to furnish workers in seasonal or other
capricious or fluctuating trades with an alternative craft.
But though the individual is greatly benefited by increasing
his versatility, it cannot be admitted that the aggregate
of employment is increased directly by any such measures.
If a painter provided with another craft sought employment
during the winter months, what craft should he possess
and where would he find employment except by displacing

another workman in that craft? Unless there are trades which are insufficiently furnished with effective labour, engaged in making goods for which the increasing demand is inadequately met, how can the new supply of labour find employment? It is of no use planning new kinds of production unless there is a sufficient growing demand to take off at a remunerative price the new products. Those who propose alternative employments for "season" workers are not prepared to point out any trades insufficiently supplied with labour, to which the season workers might have recourse.

§ 22. Sound Distribution of Public and Private Work.

In the analysis of causes of unemployment it was pointed out that in many trades there was a needless amount of irregularity of employment. In many cases orders would be distributed over a longer period of time and work would be more regular, if legislative enactments or private agreement in the trade imposed restrictions upon the hours of labour and overtime worked by all competitors. Though the intelligence and goodwill of single employers may do something to distribute employment more evenly over the year and to throw extra work of repairs, etc., on the times when general work is slack, it is clear that not much can be effected by this means. Neither can public bodies, so far as they act on ordinary business principles, throw any great increase of employment on the periods when many men are out of work. It is natural enough that either public or private employers in executing work which can be done equally well at any time, should choose those times when larger numbers of men competent to do such work are available. So if drains have to be cleared or repaired, if roads have to be made or indoor repairs executed, it is reasonable and businesslike to have this work done when plenty of suitable labour can be got, and a public body keenly acting in the public interest would select such times. Since public bodies are not always businesslike, it is legitimate for the Local Government Board to remind them of the duty of executing their business on truly economical principles. The small attention paid by municipal authorities to the advice of the central government may be attributed to a consciousness that they are already doing all that could be reasonably done to supply employment at slack times.

§ 23. Theory of Public Relief Works.

Such a businesslike disposition of public work must be carefully distinguished from all that partakes of relief works. Whenever it is claimed that public bodies should "make" work, or should give necessary work at times other than the most convenient, or should give it to workers who are not chosen for their competency, it is evident that what is done must be regarded as relief works and not classed with ordinary public work. The inability of large numbers of workers to provide adequately against trade depressions which they cannot foresee and against seasonal employment in many low-paid trades, is now widely recognised, and it is urged by many that considerations of public utility demand that public relief works should be organised which may abate the misery and the degradation of industrial character which is inseparable from long periods of unemployment.

§ 24. *Right Economic Conditions of Relief Works.*

Three tolerably obvious economic rules should guide the organisation of such relief works, where they are deemed necessary.

First, the product of the labour employed on public relief works should not be brought into competition with the products of outside labour.

Secondly, the wages paid should be somewhat lower than those paid for similar work in the outside market.

Thirdly, the work should, so far as possible, be adapted to the circumstances and the capacity of the individuals relieved, *e.g.*, a stenographer or a working jeweller should not be set to do the work of a navvy.

The validity of the first two rules will only be contested by those who seek by relief work to provide for the growth of a surreptitious and an uneconomical form of state-socialism. All relief works are of course socialistic in the sense that they form a part of that definite social support which the State deems it expedient to give to certain of its members who are unable without it to live in a condition consistent with public safety and with public self-respect. But it is of urgent importance to recognise the folly of endeavouring to build a system of public industry upon the foundation of such relief works. If in contravention to the first of the above-mentioned rules, municipal bakeries were started, not for the sake of providing cheaper and better food to consumers, but of giving employment to bakers who were out of work, one of two results would reasonably follow. If the municipal bakery paid the same or higher wages than outside bakeries, it would gradually induce the employees in the

latter to throw up their posts in order to qualify by
"unemployment" for work in the municipal bakery. If
the municipal bakery stood by its theory and admitted
all qualified applicants, it would be compelled to enlarge
its operations until it had absorbed the whole local trade.
If, on the other hand, the municipal wages were much
lower than the wages outside, and no profits were required
for the public capital and management, it is conceivable
that the municipal loaf might undersell the outside loaf.
In any case the increase of the supply of bread by the
addition of the municipal loaves would bring down the
price of bread, and increasing the congestion of supply
would make trade impossible for the weaker bakers. Thus
it appears that the establishment of a municipal bakery
could not reduce and might easily increase the unemployment of bakers: it could only absorb the unemployed
by absorbing the whole trade.   Some socialists acknowledge
this and base their advocacy of municipal workshops
chiefly on the supposition that they would lead to the
organisation of the several industries by the municipality.
More thoughtful reformers, however, repudiate this line of
movement, because they perceive that to try socialistic
experiments with workers who are selected for incapacity
in trades which are lowly organised, will ensure prompt
and signal failure. This lesson has been taught in history
over and over again, one of the most dramatic illustrations
being afforded by the attempt to establish public works
in Paris under the Commune of 1848.

§ 25. True and False Ideas of Public Industry and Employment.

If it is desirable to extend the area of State or mu-

nicipal control over industry, the highly organised routine
trades, already in the hands of large capitalist companies,
and often partaking of the character of monopolies, furnish
the more favourable field for such social experiments. To
begin by "socialising" the irregular and backward industries simply means a futile attempt to force progress
by shoving in the thick end of the wedge. Moreover it
is a sound principle to recognise that since industry
exists ultimately for the benefit of the consumer, it is his
interest and not that of the worker which should be kept
directly in view when it is proposed to assume an industry
under public management. This principle is not antago-
nistic to the adoption of "relief works" for the unemployed. But when a municipality decides that it is to the
public interest to meet some unforeseen depression of
employment by offering public wage-work upon conditions
less obnoxious and degrading than Poor Law relief, it
should do so with a clear understanding that it is depart-
ing from the ordinary rules of public business, and should
confine its experiments within the narrowest limits consistent with the provision of effective relief. To concede
any general demand to the effect that all unemployed
workers should be provided with public work at their
special trade, paid at standard wages, would mean an
attempt to reverse the national historic order of social
reconstruction, and to move towards the new industrial
order along a line of greatest possible resistance. So long as
periods of unemployment recur, which cannot be foreseen
or provided against by large numbers of workers, it is
desirable that the organised community shall take measures
by means of public work and wages to secure the suffer-
ers against the damage to life and industrial character

which such periods of enforced idleness involve. But the utmost care must be taken to absolutely sever such public employment and its product from the general current of outside industry, and to ensure that all employment afforded by public bodies in these times of distress shall be regarded as a temporary expedient justified by special social needs and not as a part of an organised attempt to reconstruct the industrial system.

§ 26. Danger of Resting upon Palliatives.

Two chief dangers beset the consideration of the specifics for unemployment here described. The first is, lest the practical reformer, impressed by the scale and importance of one or more of these schemes, should allow his mind to rest contented on a plane of palliatives, ignoring the need of more fundamental economic remedies. Linked closely with this is the tendency to impute validity to all reforms which make in the first instance for an apparent increase of employment without considering whether they are attended by an increase of the aggregate consumption. The attempt to cure unemployment by making new employments will of necessity prove futile, unless the conditions of the new employments are such as to throw an increased power of consumption into the hands of those who will use it to raise the general level of consumption in the community. This policy alone can furnish a guarantee for the steady continuance of an enlarged volume of industry and of employment.

INDEX.

www.ingramcontent.com/pod-product-compliance
Lightning Source LLC
Chambersburg PA
CBHW030333270326
41926CB00010B/1609